What Happens When Women Say Yes to God

DEVOTIONAL

LYSA TERKEURST

HARVEST HOUSE PUBLISHERS
EUGENE, OREGON

Cover by Connie Gabbert

Published in association with the literary agency of Fedd & Company, Inc., PO Box 341973, Austin, TX 78734.

WHAT HAPPENS WHEN WOMEN SAY YES TO GOD DEVOTIONAL
Copyright © 2013 by Lysa TerKeurst
Published by Harvest House Publishers
Eugene, Oregon 97408
www.harvesthousepublishers.com

ISBN 978-0-7369-7262-8 (Flexbind)
ISBN 978-0-7369-5458-7 (eBook)

Printed in China

21 22 23 24 25 26 / RDS-JC / 10 9 8 7 6

Contents

1

My Story

*You intended to harm me, but God intended it for good
to accomplish what is now being done,
the saving of many lives.*

GENESIS 50:20

🌿 Thought for the Day:

God untangled my need for approval with the challenge to live for an audience of One.

WHENEVER I'VE STEPPED OUT to do something I felt God calling me to do, the voices of criticism and condemnation have been there to greet me. Early on in ministry the voices were loud and cruel. "You'll never be a speaker." "You are not wanted." "Look at you. Do you really think God could use someone like you?"

Sometimes I measured myself against other people. "She's so clever. She's so educated. She's so connected. Who am I compared to all that?" Gradually, I shrank back. I pulled away. I put up a front of perfection with carefully crafted words and a house and kids that looked just right. Polished on the outside yet completely undone on the inside.

Eventually the Lord called my bluff. He's good at that. I was simultaneously going through the books *Experiencing God* by Henry Blackaby and *Victory Over the Darkness* by Neil Anderson. Often I would have tears stream from my eyes while attempting to get through the lessons. But one day it was more than just tears. It was sobs pouring from a chest so heavy with burdens I thought I might literally break apart.

Down on my face, I asked God to speak to me. What I heard in reply was one simple yet life-changing question: "Will you share your story?"

"Yes, I will share my story. The good parts. The parts that are safe and tidy and acceptable."

But safe and tidy and acceptable were not what God was looking for. He wanted the impossible.

Totally impossible.

Absolutely impossible…in my strength.

But God wouldn't drop it. He met every one of my arguments with Scriptures about relying not on my strength but on Him. He untangled my need for approval with the challenge to live for an audience of One. He helped me see where the voices of doubt were coming from and challenged me to consider the source. And, quite simply, He kept whispering He loved me over and over again.

The first time I shared my story was nothing but an act of absolute obedience. I kept my head down and my guard up. I expected the ladies listening to all start stoning me…especially when I got to the part about my abortion. The shame of all the abuse and rejection was nothing compared to the shame of my choice to abort my child.

I'd wept over that choice.

I'd repented.

I'd gone to God hundreds of times and asked for forgiveness. I'd laid it down every time there was an altar call. But nothing brought the redemption that this day brought. As I stood shaking at that podium, I shared exactly what and how God asked me to share.

And then the miracle happened.

When I finished and dared to look up at their reactions, tearstained faces were looking back at me. Mouths were whispering, "Me too. Me too." In that moment, I finally understood "what Satan means for evil, God can use for good."

Seeing God use the very thing that made me feel utterly worthless to help others changed everything. I was finally free from Satan's chains of shame and could see his lies for what they were.

In that moment, I felt victorious—not in my own power, but in the Lord's strength and ability to use all things for good. Without that decision of obedience, I would not have been able to see how God wanted to work in the lives of so many women that night. My saying yes to God gave others the courage to say yes to Him as well. Burdens were lifted. Lives were changed. Hidden secrets were touched by grace. It's a beautiful thing when women say yes to God. In what way is He calling you to say yes?

Dear Lord, thank You for making the impossible, possible. Thank You for taking every event in my life and using it for good. You are worthy to be praised. In Jesus' name, amen.

Reflect and Respond:

What has God placed on your heart to share with others?

Be intentional in encouraging someone with a compliment, positive note, or text message today. The Lord uses our words and actions in our own lives as well as in the lives of others.

2

God's Communication Channel

*The gatekeeper opens the gate for him, and the sheep listen to
his voice. He calls his own sheep by name and leads them out.
When he has brought out all his own, he goes on ahead of
them, and his sheep follow him because they know his voice.*

JOHN 10:3-4

Thought for the Day:

When we invest in spending time alone with God, He will speak
to us, and what we hear from Him in these quiet times will be
echoed in other places.

DO YOU SPEND TIME alone with God? We shouldn't wait to
hear from Him just on Sunday mornings or during a weekly Bible
study or when a speaker comes to town. These are places to confirm
what we've heard in our time alone, where we are personally studying God's Word, learning more about His character, and listening
for His voice.

Oh, what joy it is to know God speaks to me! But I've found
that many believers are missing this vital element in their relationship with Him. As I've talked with people about my own radical

obedience journey, they are quick to ask how they might hear from God too. Maybe you have some of these same questions: How do I know if God is speaking to me? How do I discern whether it is His voice speaking or just my own idea? What if I feel God is telling me to do something that doesn't seem to make sense?

There is no magic formula for being able to discern God's voice. We can *learn* to recognize it the way we recognize the voices of those close to us: by knowing Him. And when we know Him, we can tell if what we're feeling led to do is from Him or not.

I'll be honest. Though I do hear from God, I've never heard His voice audibly. When God speaks to me, it is a certain impression on my heart that I've come to recognize as Him. I've also learned to ask five key questions to help me determine if what I'm hearing is from God or not:

1. Does what I'm hearing line up with Scripture?
2. Is it consistent with God's character?
3. Is it being confirmed through messages I'm hearing at church or studying in my quiet times?
4. Is it beyond me?
5. Would it please God?

Asking these questions helps me tell the difference between my thoughts and God's impressions. However, we must be careful to always remember these questions are only a starting place…a guide to consider. Ultimately, God wants our ability to know His voice to come out of our close relationship with Him. Look at today's verse. Now let's reread this verse with some clarifying remarks added in.

> The gatekeeper [Jesus] opens the gate [a way for us to have direct communication with God] for him, and the sheep [you and I] listen to his voice. He [God] calls his own sheep by name [He speaks to us personally] and leads them out [providing us with direction]. When he has brought out all his own, he goes on ahead of them, and his sheep follow him because they know his voice [they know His voice because they have spent time with him] (John 10:3-4).

Jesus is the one who provides a way for us to be able to talk with God and hear from God. God calls us by name. He wants to have a personal connection with each of us. Think about when you call someone's name. You know that person. You are calling on them so the two of you can connect in some way. This verse is telling us that the way God wants to connect with us is to provide direction for us in life. He has gone before us and sees the dangers and trials we will face. He is telling us the way to go, the perspectives to keep, the things to avoid, and the things to hold fast to. Most of all, He is speaking to us because we are His own and He wants a relationship with us. He loves us, adores us, treasures us, and has a good plan for us. He longs for us to know His voice and listen to His voice. The only way to know and trust God in this way is to spend time with Him.

I never want to be outside of God's communication channel. I want to yearn every day for the things He is trying to teach me. The fact that He places this message in everything I see is a sweet confirmation of the way He is faithfully leading me. And I wouldn't have it any other way.

Dear Lord, I love how You communicate Your Word to me wherever I go. Speak to my heart today in my quiet time with You. In Jesus' name, amen.

🌿 Reflect and Respond:

How do you spend quiet time with God?

Try switching up your quiet time techniques. For example, if you love to run, spend some time in prayer as you go for a morning jog. If you're a busy mom with little ones, try sitting down with your Bible and a cup of coffee while the kids are napping.

3

Hearing God's Voice

Do not conform to the pattern of this world,
but be transformed by the renewing of your mind.
Then you will be able to test and approve
what God's will is—his good, pleasing and perfect will.

ROMANS 12:2

🌿 Thought for the Day:

Just as God always speaks in accordance with His Word, He speaks in accordance with His character.

SOMETIMES WE THINK WE hear it—the still, small voice of God. Helping us. Guiding us through a situation. Telling us what path we should take. However, there are also times where we aren't sure where that message is coming from—it could be from God or it could sprout from our own desires. It could even be Satan disguising himself to ensure we falter.

But there are a few ways we can use to decipher who, or what, is slipping those whispers into our daily decision making. Yesterday, we looked at five key questions to help us determine if what we're hearing is from God or not. Today, let's unpack two of those in greater detail.

God Will Not Speak to Us or Tell Us to Do Something Contrary to His Word

God will never contradict Himself. However, unless we know Scripture, we will not be able to discern whether what we are hearing is consistent or not with the Word. God's Word is the language the Holy Spirit uses to help us understand what God is speaking to our heart. We must get into God's Word and let God's Word get into us. This will transform our mind and prepare it for whatever God wants to tell us. Then we will be able to test and approve not just God's good will, and not just His pleasing will, but His perfect will (Romans 12:2).

The good news is that you don't need a seminary degree to read your Bible. If reading God's Word is new for you, choose a translation that is easy to understand with a built-in commentary. A good rule of thumb is "simply start and start simply." Read a passage of Scripture today and ask yourself

- Who is this passage speaking to?
- What is it saying to me?
- What direction is this passage giving?
- How might I need to change my way of thinking or acting as a result of this verse?
- What are some other verses that relate to this topic, both in the Old Testament and New Testament?

God's Word Provides Rich Information Regarding His Character

As you come across verses revealing aspects of God's nature, make note of them. Just as God always speaks in accordance with

His Word, He speaks in accordance with His character. God will not say things that are inconsistent with who He is. The apostle Paul writes, "Those who live according to the flesh have their minds set on what the flesh desires; but those who live in accordance with the Spirit have their minds set on what the Spirit desires" (Romans 8:5). What is it that God's Spirit desires? Answering this question helps us understand God's character.

We find great insight into God's character in Galatians 5:22-23: "The fruit of the Spirit is love, joy, peace, forbearance [patience], kindness, goodness, faithfulness, gentleness and self-control." These characteristics in a person's life are the evidence of Christ at work.

> The fruit of the Spirit is the spontaneous work of the Holy Spirit in us. The Spirit produces these character traits that are found in the nature of Christ. They are by-products of Christ's control—we can't obtain them by trying to get them without his help. If we want the fruit of the Spirit to grow in us, we must join our lives to his. We must know him, love him, remember him, and imitate him. [1]

If the fruit of the Spirit is our imitation of Him, then it must be consistent with God's character.

When you feel God speaking to you, ask yourself: Is what I am hearing consistent with God's love, joy, peace, etc.?

In addition to the fruit of the Spirit, God's character is revealed in a loving relationship with us. As we experience God personally, we come to know new names for Him. When we've experienced His provision, we come to know Him as our Provider. When we've experienced His comfort, we come to know Him as our Comforter.

When we've experienced His amazing love, we come to know Him as the Great Lover of our souls. The longer we know Him and the more we experience Him personally, the more we learn about His character.

We are truly blessed to serve a God who fights for us to hear His voice above the deafening messages we receive from the world. It's so important to listen up, tune in, and prepare our hearts for what He has to say. If we're too busy listening to other sources, we just might miss the most important whisper ever spoken to us.

Dear Lord, thank You for giving me the tools to see Your desires for me. Through Your Word and what I know about Your character, I can recognize where that small voice is coming from. I love You, Lord, and want to please You. In Jesus' name, amen.

🌿 Reflect and Respond:

Answer some of the questions mentioned in today's devotion. This will help you discern whether or not what you're hearing/feeling is coming from God.

Start a journal. Record the verses you study and some of the personal experiences with things you are learning as you read God's Word.

4

God's Calling

*I am the LORD your God
who takes hold of your right hand and says to you,
Do not fear; I will help you.*

ISAIAH 41:13

🌿 **Thought for the Day:**

The beauty of doing things beyond ourselves is that we will know it was by God's doing and His alone.

WHEN GOD LEADS OR prompts us to do something small, we will be able to do it if we're willing.

But sometimes He calls us to do something big, and we feel we can't do it in our own strength because it is either beyond our ability or beyond our natural human desire.

It is not something we can strategize and manipulate into being in and of ourselves. It can only happen by God's divine intervention. The beauty of doing things beyond ourselves is that we will know it was by God's doing and His alone. And to Him we give all the glory.

I remember when God called me to write my first book. It seemed so exciting and thrilling to think of accomplishing this huge life goal. I envisioned the cover with my name on it. I delighted in imagining the first time I would walk into a bookstore and quietly say to myself, "I wrote that." The excitement carried me through writing the first 10,000 words. Everything was clicking right along... until I got a note from my editor after she read my first installment. Her two-page, single-spaced feedback can be summed up in two shocking words: "Start over."

I got down on the floor beside my desk, buried my face in the carpet, and cried. "I can't do this, God. I can't write a whole book. What was I thinking? I'm not an author. I'm an imposter who some-how got lucky enough to fool this publisher with my proposal. But now they've seen the real me and think I'm a fool."

Did you notice an often-repeated word in my cries to God? "I'm not." "I can't." "I'm a fool." It was all about me and my inadequacies until I turned the statements into "God is." "God can." "God has called me; therefore, I am equipped."

If God is calling you to do something you feel is beyond you, you are in good company. God has a history of calling people to things that were beyond themselves. Pastor Rick Warren put it this way

> Abraham was old, Jacob was insecure, Leah was unattractive, Joseph was abused, Moses stuttered, Gideon was poor, Samson was codependent, Rahab was immoral, David had an affair and all kinds of family problems, Elijah was suicidal, Jeremiah was depressed, Jonah was reluctant, Naomi was a widow, John the Baptist was eccentric to say the least, Peter

was impulsive and hot-tempered, Martha worried a lot, the Samaritan woman had several failed marriages, Zachaeus was unpopular, Thomas had doubts, Paul had poor health, and Timothy was timid. That's quite a group of misfits, but God used each of them in his service. He will use you too. [1]

Don't look at your inabilities and dwell in insecurities. Look at the Almighty God. See this call as the opportunity to watch Him work in you and through you. If you answer yes to the question "Is this beyond me?" chances are God is speaking.

It's easy to talk ourselves out of thinking we've heard from God. I think we'll pretty much use any excuse to convince ourselves it's not His voice so we don't need to act. But there's one very important question to ask when we feel prompted to do something, one question that takes away our excuses: Would this please God? You see, if what you are doing pleases God, then even if what you thought you heard from Him wasn't His voice, you still please Him. We should always seek to err on the side of pleasing God.

The more you practice listening for God's voice, the more it becomes a natural part of your daily life. And here's the best news of all: God wants you to hear Him. He wants your faith to grow. He wants you to surrender all and whisper "Yes."

Dear Lord, You are able and mighty. I am so grateful for the calling You have placed on my life. I pray You will continue to use me and teach me to rely on Your ability instead of my own. In Jesus' name, amen.

Reflect and Respond:

What is God calling you to today? Spend some quiet time with Him in the Word. Listen for His voice, and let Him speak to your heart.

5

The Secret Place

Remain in me, as I also remain in you.
No branch can bear fruit by itself;
it must remain in the vine. Neither can you
bear fruit unless you remain in me.

JOHN 15:4

Thought for the Day:

To remain in Him and enter the secret place, I simply have to close my eyes and make the choice to be with God.

CAN I LET YOU in on something? There is a place I escape to that allows my soul to breathe and rest and reflect. It is the place where I can drop the "yuck" the world hands me and trade it in for the fullness of God. It is a place where God reassures me, confirms He has everything under control, and gives me a new filter through which I can process life.

John 15:4 says, "Remain in me, as I also remain in you. No branch can bear fruit by itself; it must remain in the vine. Neither can you bear fruit unless you remain in me." This peaceful and fruitful remaining place is my secret place.

Let's be honest. It's hard for a well-meaning soul that desires radical obedience to God to live in a body made of flesh.

Our flesh is pulled by the distractions of the world, lured to sell our soul for temporary pleasures and conned by Satan's schemes. Other people rub us the wrong way, and we instantly want to give them a piece of our mind. Worldly wealth screams that if only you could do more to have more, then ultimate happiness could be yours. And our right to be right seems to supersede the sacrificial call of God.

All the while God invites our souls to break away from the world and remain in Him. To remain in Him and enter the secret place, I simply have to close my eyes and make the choice to be with God.

Sometimes I do this because I'm in a desperate place. I pray, "God, I am here and I need You right now. I'm feeling attacked, invaded, pressed, and stressed. Meet me here and help me process what I'm facing using Your truth. Nothing more and nothing less. I don't want this thing I'm facing to be processed through my selfish and insecure flesh. I will surely act in a displeasing and dishonoring way if I'm left to face this on my own. Block my flesh's natural reaction and fill me with Your Spirit. You handle this for me. You speak what needs to be spoken and give power to hold my tongue for what needs to be left in silence."

Other times I need to be with God because I'm feeling pulled into something I know is not part of His best plan for me. I see something new I can't afford. How easy it is to justify our way to the checkout line, whip out a credit card, and decide to deal with the consequences later. Or maybe it is a relationship we know is not in God's will. Or a particular eating habit we know is not healthy for us.

Whatever it is, we don't have to be rendered powerless by this pull. We can pray, "God, I know You are more powerful than this pull I am feeling. I know this thing I think I want so much will only provide temporary pleasure. I know the consequences of making this choice will rob me of joy and peace in the near future. Through Your power I am making the choice to walk away. I will find my delight in You and look forward to feeling Your fullness replace the emptiness this desire creates."

Still other times I simply know I need a fresh filling of God's Spirit in me. I go to this secret place and simply talk to God. Then I listen for His voice. Sometimes He provides direction and instruction on something that needs to be done. Other times I sense Him warning me of something coming. Still other times He simply lavishes me with His love.

I love saying yes to God and going to the secret place with Him.

God clearly tells us in John 15:4 that this is the only way to bear fruit in our lives. It is the only way to experience what Galatians 5:22-23 (NASB) explains this fruit to be: love, joy, peace, patience, kindness, goodness, faithfulness, gentleness, and self-control. Oh, how I want these to be the character of my heart and the legacy of my life.

Obedience is the key that unlocks this secret place with God.

John 15:10 goes on to explain this, "If you keep my commands, you will remain in my love." The more we say yes to God, the more we will live in expectation of seeing Him. The more we expect to see God, the more we will. The more you experience Him, the more you'll trust Him. The more you trust Him, the more you'll open up your hands in absolute obedience.

Dear Lord, I am so thankful for the secret place, where I can let my soul rest in You. I know You are more powerful than any pressure or worldly pull in the wrong direction that I feel. Help me to be obedient and to remain in You above all else. In Jesus' name, amen.

Reflect and Respond:

Do you regularly spend time with God? If so, don't let it become just another thing on your to-do list. Ensure it is still a renewing experience by eliminating any activities you would typically do before your moments alone with God.

If you aren't coming before God daily, make it a point to do this first thing in the morning. As you spend more and more time in His presence, it will be something that naturally occurs in strengthening your relationship with Him.

6

A Year of Adventure

---

*Great is your faithfulness. I say to myself,
"The LORD is my portion; therefore I will wait for him."*

LAMENTATIONS 3:23-34

Thought for the Day:

The adventure is waiting.

WHEN MY YOUNGEST DAUGHTER was in the seventh grade, she presented my husband and me with a proposal. An iMovie proposal. Complete with dramatic scenes and credits that rolled at the end.

The message of the iMovie? A request. "Please homeschool me."

Oh, my heavenly days, no.

No.

No.

No. I'm not a teacher.

No. I'm not patient.

No. I'm not even nice some days.

No.

I had tried homeschooling this darling in kindergarten, and I honestly thought I was going to lose my mind. I would watch other moms do this thing right. They were organized and scheduled and undistracted.

Me? I looked like the tongue of a dog when he's got his head stuck out the window of a truck going 70 miles per hour. Messy. Flapping about. Not pretty to look at.

Can you imagine the conversations she will have about me with her therapist one day? No, let's not add homeschooling to the list of things Mom didn't do well.

But then I got to thinking. (You know those 3:00 a.m. thinking times when you should be sleeping but can't? Yes, I started having lots of those.) What if I just took a year of adventure with this beautiful young woman? What if I just hit the pause button on all things typical and just took a year to do things differently? With her. For her. Could I do that?

Okay, God. If You want me to take a year of adventure with Brooke, show me.

Then I met a math teacher who got all excited about coming to my house to teach her math a couple times a week. And then a fabulous reading and writing tutor just happened to have a couple days a week to do the same.

My friend Kate asked if Brooke could be in her small-group Bible study this year. Another friend asked if Brooke wanted to take cheerleading classes at her gym. And I'd already been planning an educational trip to Sea World.

So the year of adventure started unfolding in front of me. "Yet this I call to mind and therefore I have hope: Because of the Lord's great love we are not consumed, for His compassions never fail. They are new every morning; great is your faithfulness. I say to myself, 'The LORD is my portion; therefore I will wait for him'" (Lamentations 3:21-24).

I had no idea how the year would turn out. I thought I might royally mess up my child's education, but it is turning out to be a year we will never forget. We are still living out the adventure. It has been wonderful. And it has been hard. (Especially the day my tutor quit because…well, sometimes seventh graders are not so interested in remembering to complete their assignments.) Wonderful and hard often go together when saying yes to God. But this year has grown us, stretched us, and brought us together.

You too can have a year of adventure with your children. Maybe it's the year of them learning 12 Bible verses—one per month. Or maybe it could be the year of each child making their bed at least 3 to 4 times per week. Or maybe it's the year of letter writing, where you have them write 1 letter per week to brighten someone's day.

You can have a year of adventure with the Lord. It can be the year you embark on the journey of saying yes to God. A time to start giving it all to Him and walking in radical obedience.

Take a leap of faith. Say yes. This year holds so much opportunity for you. The adventure is waiting!

Dear Lord, thank You for the opportunity to stretch myself in ways I never thought possible. Even though the idea of this scares me, I know You will provide everything I need to get through the good and the bad days. Please use this as an opportunity for me to grow closer to You. In Jesus' name, amen.

🌿 Reflect and Respond:

Think about what your year of adventure would look like if you chose to say yes. What kind of adventurous thing could you do this year? Start with something small. One thing. It doesn't have to be complicated, but should be something outside of your comfort zone that will stretch you.

7

A Party in Your Honor

---

*It is God who works in you to will and to act
in order to fulfill his good purpose.*

PHILIPPIANS 2:13

❧ Thought for the Day:

Saying yes to God isn't about perfect performance, but rather perfect surrender to the Lord day by day.

IMAGINE YOU'RE PLANNING A wonderful surprise party for someone you dearly love. You've made the plans, invited all the guests, and decided on an exquisite menu. You can't wait for the big moment when all the guests yell, "Surprise!" and your loved one finally joins in the festivities. You know she'll understand just how cherished and adored she is when she sees everything that's been done in her honor.

Finally, the time for the surprise arrives. All of the guests are waiting in anticipation at the front door. You see your loved one pull into the driveway, and you hear the car engine turn off. As she opens the car door, you see the interior lights come on while she gathers her things. Your heart races as you see her heading up the driveway. Suddenly, she makes an unusual turn and heads to the back door.

You quickly make your way to the back door to redirect her. Your cheerful greeting is met with a halfhearted smile, and your attempts to send her to the front door are brushed aside. She insists she is tired and will look at what you want to show her tomorrow. Only you know that tomorrow the guests will be gone, the leftover food will be stored away, and the party will be over.

How sad for the guest of honor who missed her own surprise party! And how disappointing for the party planner who orchestrated the event.

God must feel the same way when we miss the "surprise parties" (the divine appointments) that await us each day. How it must disappoint Him when we don't hear or don't listen to Him redirecting us to the front door. How it must grieve Him when we walk through our lives oblivious of His activity all around us. How it must break His heart when we brush aside something that not only would make us feel special and noticed by God, but also would allow us to join Him in making life a little sweeter for others.

How many times have we missed our own surprise party?

God reveals Himself and His activity to all of us, but very few really want an encounter with Him. Encounters cause extreme changes in our plans, our perspectives, and our personhood, and most of us hate change. In reality, though, the very act of trying to protect ourselves from change is the very thing that makes our life the boring mess that it sometimes is.

As I've traveled around the country speaking at conferences, I am amazed and saddened by the number of people missing out on the most exciting part of being a Christian—experiencing God. Over and over people tell me they want something more in their Christian life. They want the kind of relationship with God where they recognize His voice, live in expectation of His activity, and embrace a life totally sold out for Him. I suspect that tucked in the corner of your heart is the same desire. And I've discovered that the key to having this kind of incredible adventure is radical obedience.

You may be surprised to discover that radical obedience is not really that radical. It is really biblical obedience, but we've strayed so far from biblical obedience that it now seems radical. In today's society, it is radical to obey God's commands, listen to the Holy Spirit's convictions, and walk in Jesus' character, but we will never experience the radical blessings God has in store for us without radical obedience. It is the road that leads to blessing. It is what happens when women say yes to God.

And you won't find the full blessing until you give walking in obedience your full attention. Obedience, however, is more than just "not sinning." It is having the overwhelming desire to walk in the center of God's will at every moment. Don't stumble over fearing you won't be perfect or that you are sure to mess up.

Saying yes to God isn't about perfect performance, but rather perfect surrender to the Lord day by day. Your obedience becomes radical the minute this desire turns into real action. Radical obedience is hearing from God, feeling His nudges, participating in His activity, and experiencing His blessings in ways few people ever do.

God is waiting for you. Waiting to bless you and lead you on your walk in radical obedience. All you need to do is redirect your focus on pleasing Him, and your life will never be the same.

So today, get excited, say yes, and let the confetti fly.

Dear Lord, I don't want to miss any more divine appointments or blessings. Show me how to say yes to You, even if it changes the plans I have made for myself. In Jesus' name, amen.

❧ Reflect and Respond:

What is God calling you to say yes to? Don't say yes out of obligation. Park your heart and mind in a place that will cultivate gratitude and a willing spirit—His Word. God wants to bless you! Get excited about His will and the plans He has for you.

8

There's No Way

*Jesus answered, "I am the way the truth and the life.
No one comes to the Father except through me."*

JOHN 14:6

 Thought for the Day:

If I let Jesus be my way, and do what He is asking me to do,
I can be a light rising in the darkness.

I WASN'T IN THE mood to be messed up.

I put my head against my bedroom wall, closed my eyes, and
whispered, "There's no way." It was late summer of 2003 when my
world collided with what seemed like an impossible invitation from
God: adopt two teen boys from war-torn Liberia.

All the reasons why this wasn't a good idea tumbled before me.
Honest reasons. Understandable reason. Solid reasons.

Who would do such a thing?

Missionaries would be much more qualified. Missionaries with
grown kids and multicultural experience. People much more spiritual than me. People much more gentle and patient enough to do
this sort of thing.

Not this disorganized woman who originally thought Liberia was in South America.

Not this mom who already felt overwhelmed with her three kids. How would we add in two more?

Not someone who couldn't find the video she rented a month ago and who paid so many late fees at the library they should have named a shelf after her. Maybe two shelves.

Definitely not me.

But it was me. The invitation was mine.

And I knew it.

No matter how many times I whispered over and over, "There's no way," a nagging sense of possibility wouldn't leave me. It wove its way through every fiber of my being until I stood up and shifted everything I thought my family would be with one weak whisper, "Yes."

I can honestly say there were moments of sheer joy where I felt reassured I'd heard God right. But there were many other moments where life felt chaotic, messy, and really hard. There were tears. There were moments where I loved my five kids but I didn't like them very much. There were moments I wondered if I'd heard God wrong.

And there were more times even after we adopted where I said, "There's no way." There was no way we could overcome a medical diagnosis one of my boys got. There was no way two teenage boys who tested at a kindergarten level could catch up in two years and be ready for middle school. There was no way I could be patient enough to educate them at home during those two years.

But every time I said, "There's no way," I'd remember Jesus calling Himself "the way" (John 14:6).

He was the way. He was the one to follow. He was the one who would guide me each day. He was the one I needed to pour out my heart to in prayer. He was the one to listen to. And He was the one who reassured me with so many promises in the Bible. One of those promises was in the book of Isaiah.

> If you spend yourselves in behalf of the hungry and satisfy the needs of the oppressed, then your light will rise in the darkness, and your night will become like the noonday. The LORD will guide you always; he will satisfy your needs in a sun-scorched land and will strengthen your frame. You will be like a well-watered garden, like a spring whose waters never fail (Isaiah 58:10-11).

I could be a light rising in the darkness. I could be full of life like a well-watered garden. I could be refreshing like a spring whose waters never fail. Me. Crazy, incapable, crying-in-my-closet me. If I let Jesus be my way and do what He was asking me to do, these things could be true for me.

And they can be true for you as well.

Do you have a situation in your life where you are saying, "There's no way"? Maybe you aren't called to adopt, but whatever you are being called to do or face, take heart. Search the Bible and find promises that apply to your situation. And follow Jesus' instruction for that promise.

My sweet friend, there might not be a way if you only look at your situation with human reasoning and calculation. But if you let Jesus' truth and promises fill you, you'll find a different way. A good way. A sure way. His way.

Dear Lord, thank You for reminding me that You are the only true way. Help me to see this every day as the circumstances of life surround and sometimes overwhelm me. I desperately need Your help as I learn to say yes to Your calling on my life. In Jesus' name, amen.

Reflect and Respond:

Have you been running a list in your head of why you are not good enough to do what God has called you to do? Write down who you are in Christ. With and through Him, we are more than capable of doing all He has called us to do.

9

Tearing Down the Impossible

"You don't have enough faith," Jesus told them. "I tell you the
truth, if you had faith even as small as a mustard seed,
you could say to this mountain, 'Move from here to there,'
and it would move. Nothing would be impossible."

MATTHEW 17:20 NLT

Thought for the Day:

All impossibilities have a weak spot. And that's the exact spot
where we must attack.

I DISTINCTLY REMEMBER THE day my dad brought home a
typewriter. His office had gotten these new machines called com-
puters. Something within me stirred and went wild at the thought
of possessing a typewriter.

I loved the way it could strike and letter up a page of nothing
and make it something.

Maybe I could write a book one day? The thought came and
delighted me until I placed my hands on the keyboard. And the
only words that came to me were all the reasons I couldn't possibly write a book.

The dream was silenced.

The same thing happened to me when the high school choir director announced we would be doing a musical. I was so excited. I could see myself playing the lead role. Until I heard my friend practicing with bold assurance and booming accuracy. Suddenly every note I sang felt painfully hollow.

The dream was silenced.

And then in my mid-twenties I dared to tell a friend I thought I might want to speak at the women's event we were planning. Originally, I was just going to help plan the event, but the stirring to speak wouldn't leave me. So I gave voice to my crazy thought.

She just tilted her head and said, "No. I feel certain you aren't supposed to speak."

The dream was silenced.

Has this ever happened to you? Voices within remind us of all the reasons we're incapable. Voices around us all seem more confident. And the voices of the naysayers are just flat out rude.

Oh, how impossibility loves to scream into gaps of silenced dreams.

But here's the thing about impossible—some part of what we're attempting isn't impossible. All impossibilities have a weak spot. And that's the exact place where we must attack.

A book might seem impossible, but that's not where writers should start anyhow. An article could be written. Or in today's world, a tweet could be crafted. Or a blog posted.

Write there. In the weak spot of impossibility. Maybe your marriage seems impossible. Go against the grain of your hurt feelings and silent brush-offs. Think on just one thing you do love about that man of yours today. Send him a text about how much you appreciate that one thing. Praise him for that one thing. Tell someone else about that one thing you noticed today.

Start there. In the weak spot of impossibility. I don't know what impossibility you might be facing today. But remember—all impossibilities have a weak spot. It's there. Ask God to show you where it is. Ask God for just enough strength to attack there. Tear it down one good decision at a time.

And soon you will see that inside every impossible is the word "possible"…if only we dare to see it.

> *Dear Lord, I am so thankful that with You anything is possible. Help me to see this in my daily life. Help me to remember that without You I will surely fail, but with Your strength in me, I will triumph. You are so good. In Jesus' name, amen.*

❧ Reflect and Respond:

What is your impossible?

Now that we have identified that, what is your impossibility's weak spot?

10

Dear God, Where Are You?

*God is our refuge and strength, an
ever-present help in trouble.*

PSALM 46:1

Thought for the Day:

Sometimes God's power is shown as much in preventing things
as it is in making them happen.

"MOM, I DIDN'T MAKE it. Please pray for me. I just feel confused about God."

My heart sank. I felt my daughter's deep hurt. I felt it as clearly
as if it were my own. I know what it feels like to want something
so badly and have that dream shut down. That door closed. That
opportunity slip away.

She'd been talking about going for this special achievement at
summer camp for three years. Every time we discussed camp, she
talked about going for this achievement. But she wasn't old enough
to try until this year; her fourth year at camp.

Finally, this was to be her year.

She met every challenge and could see the goal in sight…until the fire. She was supposed to light a campfire with nothing but three matches, one small square of newspaper, and a few sticks of wood.

She struck the first match and held it up to the newspaper. It didn't ignite. She struck the second match and held it up to the newspaper. It still didn't ignite.

She stared at the third and final match. Knowing that a big part of the challenge was teaching the kids how to communicate with God and fully rely on Him, she'd been praying through every stage of the challenge. But now she didn't just pray—she cried out to God.

"Please help me, God. Please," she mouthed as she struck the third match. She held the flame up to the paper once again and watched in complete disbelief. The matchstick burned but the paper did not.

As soon as the final match burned out, she lowered her head in defeat and gave all her wood to the girls still in.

There were nine girls going for this achievement. Six girls were crowned with the highest honor at camp for finishing the challenge. Three girls didn't make it, including my daughter.

When I arrived at camp to pick her up a week later, she asked if we could go sit by ourselves and process this situation. What was bothering her wasn't the missed chance of getting the camp honor. No, what upset her the most was *not* experiencing God's power the way the other girls did. They all had stories of God answering their cries for help in amazing ways that carried them all the way through the challenge.

"Mom, I didn't get that with God. Why?"

This was a tough question. One of those questions that, as a mom, you don't want to mess up when answering.

I asked her to help me recall every step of her challenge so we could intentionally look for God's hand. As she recalled every part, I listened intently for anything unusual and unexplainable.

And when she got to the fire, I found it. There was no reason her newspaper shouldn't have lit. None at all. Everyone else's paper lit. Hers should have. But it didn't.

"Honey, that can only be explained by God intervening. He was there. He was listening. And we just have to trust that there was some reason you shouldn't have continued that challenge. We may not know that reason, but we can certainly trust God was right there...protecting you...loving you...revealing His power to you."

She put her head on my shoulder, "You really think so, Mom?"

I whispered, "I know so."

I know so because I trust the truth God has given me. Truths like these are anchors that hold me to the reality of who God is.

He is the One in whom I find comfort and reassurance. "I have told you these things, so that in me you may have peace. In this world you will have trouble. But take heart! I have overcome the world" (John 16:33).

He is right here with me in the midst of my trouble. I am not alone. "God is our refuge and strength, an ever-present help in trouble" (Psalm 46:1).

He is the One who can use my tears to water the soil of my heart so that it can one day be a harvest of joy. "Those who sow with tears will reap with songs of joy" (Psalm 126:5)

Yes, I know deep hurt, but I also know deep hope. So I whispered it again, "Yes, sweetheart, I know so."

Sometimes God's power is shown as much in preventing things

as it is in making them happen. We may never know why, but we can always know and trust the Who.

Dear Lord, thank You for knowing what I need and what I don't—even when I don't agree. Teach me to trust You and look for Your hand in every situation. Help me see Your yes and Your no as protection and guidance. Today, I choose to trust You. In Jesus' name, amen.

🌿 Reflect and Respond:

Look back at a situation in which you felt God didn't answer your prayers. Can you see His power in not allowing your prayer to be answered? Be specific. It's important to acknowledge God's provision and protection.

Write out your prayer today. Focus on trusting who God is instead of why He is choosing not to answer or to delay His response. Remind yourself, "God's power is shown as much in preventing things as it is in making them happen."

11

Why I'm Breaking Up with My Quiet Time

You, God, are my God, earnestly I seek you;
I thirst for you, my whole being longs for you,
in a dry and parched land where there is no water.

PSALM 63:1

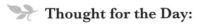 **Thought for the Day:**

When God becomes routine rather than revival, it's time to switch things up.

I'M TAKING A BREAK from having a quiet time because sometimes I can get in a rut—even with good things. And having a daily quiet time is a good thing. That is, until it becomes more about routine than actually connecting with God.

When God becomes routine rather than revival, it's time to switch things up.

Otherwise, I might start seeing this time as less important. It becomes the second or third thing I do. After other things. Seemingly more pressing things. Before I know it, it's been days since I connected privately and personally with Truth.

And then my soul feels a bit off and sluggish. Like when my stomach has been denied food, a desperation starts creeping over other parts of my body. That happens with soul hunger too.

Only the triggers for stomach hunger are much more apparent. My brain quickly reminds me, "You feel awful because you need to eat."

Sometimes my brain isn't as quick to pick up on soul hunger. So I just lumber forward but wonder, "What's wrong?" I think of a list of reasons…I'm tired, I haven't had enough fun, or my butt looks big in these jeans.

And while some of those things may be true, it's not why I feel off. I need more time with God.

Not more quiet time. More listening time.

Like the writer in Psalm 63:1 needed. "You, God, are my God, earnestly I seek you; I thirst for you, my whole being longs for you, in a dry and parched land where there is no water."

Because when I spend more time listening to Him, I am able to discern when He is calling me to action. Calling me to submit to His will with radical obedience.

One morning as I sat with God with nothing but willingness to listen, three things popped into my mind. I can't say "God spoke to me," but it felt right. I need to do some new things as I listen.

1. *Study wisdom by reading a chapter in Proverbs every day.* I ask God to reveal my verse for the day and think of ways to apply it. Ways I can share what I've learned so that it will bless others. I listen.

2. *Read something from someone I admire.* I need to study leadership in this season of my life. So I pick up a book

written on this topic by someone I admire and glean
from their wisdom. I listen.

3. *Read something from someone I trust.* A book I'm reading
   right now is whimsical and grounded all at the same
   time. It makes me feel that this writer gets me. They get
   my struggles and offer up advice I know I can trust. I
   listen.

Maybe you think all of this still sounds like a quiet time, but to
me it's different. It's a listening time. A time to shake things up a bit
and get outside my normal routine. It's a time to listen to God speak.
And He does speak…through His book of wisdom, through someone I admire, and through someone I trust.

And now? My soul feels that thrilling and comforting full feeling. Complete. Satisfied. Deeply nourished.

Dear Lord, I'm seeking to grow a stronger relationship with
You today. Help me to break out of the routine so I can connect
with You and hear You speak. In Jesus' name, amen.

🪶 Reflect and Respond:

What do you need to break up with so you can connect more
closely and listen more intently to God?

Write a list of things you are placing as priorities before your time
with God. Consider how to prioritize so God comes first.

12

If It Were Easy, It Wouldn't Be Worth Doing

---

*We know that in all things
God works for the good of those who love him,
who have been called according to his purpose.*

Romans 8:28

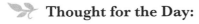 **Thought for the Day:**

Purpose and perspective lead to the perseverance that is evident in those living a truly devoted life.

I WAS DISCOURAGED.

In two months' time my life went from being wonderfully fulfilling and clicking right along to being completely topsy-turvy.

My computer went on the blink and some very important documents disappeared.

A big book deal I was excited about fell through.

Our well broke, and we had to go several days without water.

A diamond fell out of my wedding ring.

Then, on top of a host of other interruptions and haphazard

happenings, my husband blew out his knee and had to have major reconstructive surgery, leaving him bedridden for nearly five weeks. I felt myself getting caught in a whirlwind of emotions.

I didn't know whether to laugh or cry. A friend of mine hit the nail on the head when she said, "Lysa, I think when you go with God to a new level, you get a new devil."

While I'm not sure about the exact theological correctness of that statement, I do know that Satan hates the radically obedient soul. He hates it when a person jumps off the fence of complacency and into the center of God's will. A spiritual battle is raging around us, and because of that life can be hard. While saying yes to God does bring blessing, it's not easy.

If our desire for obedience is born merely out of duty, we may be quick to give up. However, if our desire is born out of delight, out of a love relationship that burns deep in our soul, it won't be extinguished—no matter the cost.

One of my favorite love stories in the Bible is that of Jacob and Rachel. Jacob's love for Rachel gave him purpose and perspective, which led to amazing persistence. He served Rachel's father for many years to earn the right to marry Rachel because he loved her that much: "Jacob served seven years to get Rachel, but they seemed like only a few days to him because of his love for her" (Genesis 29:20).

Do you see what love can do for a person's view of his circumstances? When you are crazy in love with someone, you'll do anything for him—and do it with the highest level of sheer joy. I want to be so crazy in love with Jesus that not only do I serve Him, but I do it with absolute delight.

A real sign of spiritual maturity is looking to God not for comfort and convenience but for purpose and perspective.

Comfort and convenience lead to complacency. When trouble comes, the complacent person becomes critical of everyone, including God. On the other hand, purpose and perspective lead to the perseverance that is evident in those living a truly devoted life. The persistent person eagerly looks to handle trials and struggles in a way that honors God and allows personal growth.

Because we love God, we look for and trust in His purpose in everything.

The persistent person understands the meaning of Romans 8:28: "We know that in all things God works for the good of those who love him, who have been called according to his purpose." This does not mean that everything that happens to us will be good, but that God will work in and through every situation to bring good from it.

And let's not miss the last four words of this verse, where we are reminded that it is all "according to his purpose." God has a purpose, and His plans to accomplish that purpose are perfect. Trusting God's good purpose, and seeking to understand that He takes all the events from our life and orchestrates good from them, leads to a changed perspective.

So although it may be difficult to maintain the right perspective with technology on the fritz and a house that hasn't been cleaned in weeks, it's important to look to God for that change in mentality. Only He can transform our hearts and attitudes. With an increased dependence on God, we can trust that in the midst of all the things that seem to be going wrong, something will go right.

Dear Lord, I praise You and thank You for the purpose You place in everything. Give me Your perspective today as I struggle with some things that may not be going "right." I know You have a greater plan through it all. In Jesus' name, amen.

❧ Reflect and Respond:

What do you need to have a better perspective on today? Write down every negative thought, and for each negative statement write a positive statement next to it. Replacing negativity with positivity will help to transform your outlook on the situation.

13

Secrets of Success Found
in Small Places

Have I not commanded you? Be strong and courageous.
Do not be afraid; do not be discouraged,
for the LORD your God will be with you wherever you go.

JOSHUA 1:9

Thought for the Day:

Rejection from man doesn't mean rejection from God.

THE INTERNATIONAL CHRISTIAN RETAILERS Show is a big book convention where publishers, authors, agents, media, and bookstore owners all gather to talk shop. Books are pitched. Books are sold. Books are talked about a lot!

I went to this conference years ago when I was just a wannabe writer with a book proposal and a dream. Recently, as I signed prerelease copies of my book *Unglued*, two thoughts were going through my mind.

The first thought was *Thank You, Jesus, that people actually came to my book signing.* Seriously, there's nothing quite like standing there with a big stack of free books, a Sharpie marker, and not an interested soul in sight.

Can you imagine the joy the publisher would feel toward me in that moment? "If we can't even give the book away, how are we going to sell it?" So when people actually came, I wanted to hug every single one of them. And if I had lots of money, I would have wanted to buy each of them a steak dinner. I'm not kidding.

The second thought was *Look for those desperate for your encouragement.* Many of the people who came through my book signing line were people interested in writing a book one day. I remember being there. I know what it feels like to walk around with a tote bag full of book proposals and a heart full of nervous hope. I felt the weight of responsibility to give them the encouragement I so desperately needed when I was in their shoes.

Maybe you are there right now. Whether it's the hope of being an author or a different dream you have bumping around in your heart, here's what I've learned.

Always remember rejection from man doesn't mean rejection from God. Joshua 1:9 teaches, "Have I not commanded you? Be strong and courageous. Do not be afraid; do not be discouraged, for the LORD your God will be with you wherever you go." We are here to do what God has called us to do. And we should not let the opinion of man define us. We need to put our hope in the Lord, the One who will never reject us or forsake us.

If God has gifted you to write, then write. You don't need a book deal to have an impact with your writing. The same is true with other dreams. Sing, create, teach, paint, lead—use your gifts right where you are to bless others.

Most overnight success stories are years in the making. Value the daily discipline of small steps, hard work, honing your craft, and putting in time learning and developing. Take classes. Be mentored. Push through those moments you want to slack off. And do it over and over, year after year.

Be a blessing to others. Don't keep your work to yourself. Find people who could be blessed with your work. I love to write, but what I love more than writing is seeing that my writing is helping other people. That's where I find the encouragement to push through the hard times.

Expect opposition. Challenges, disappointments, and setbacks are all part of the experience. And honestly, these hard times serve a great purpose. I think I've learned much more from my failures in writing than in my successes. Just remember to use these lessons… don't waste them by giving up too soon. And remember to glorify God whether it's a struggle or a success. He uses all things for good. "We are God's handiwork, created in Christ Jesus to do good works, which God prepared in advance for us to do" (Ephesians 2:10).

Look for the small open doors right in front of you. I always scratch my head when I meet people who tell me they want to write and speak but aren't willing to teach a small Bible study first. If God is calling you to do something, He'll have a door open in front of you, but it might be a small door. Look for the small door and walk through it.

Actually, dance through it with great joy because He will always do great things with people willing to be faithful and radically obedient in the small things.

Dear Lord, thank You for giving me the opportunity to pursue my dreams. I am so humbled that You would call me to serve You. Please help me persevere as I come up against oppo-sition and frustration in the process of saying yes to You. In Jesus' name, amen.

❧ Reflect and Respond:

What small step can you take in reaching your goal? Remember, we can't go from A to Z. There are many stepping-stones along the way. Surround yourself with a positive support network. Having a strong group of friends and family who will stand with you and be honest with you on your journey is crucial.

14

No Matter What

Rejoice always, pray continually,
give thanks in all circumstances;
for this is God's will for you in Christ Jesus.

1 Thessalonians 5:16-18

🌿 Thought for the Day:

We can settle in our hearts that we will choose God's love and the pursuit of a love relationship with Him above all else.

THERE ARE SOME THINGS God wants us to get settled in our hearts. Do we want to chase after the world's emptiness instead of His fullness? Or do we want our lives to be characterized by perfect love instead of perfect performance?

Many people halfheartedly claim to be Christians, believing that because we will never be perfect this side of eternity we have an excuse to pursue that which pleases our human longings. Why not push the limits, live for the now, and worry about eternity later?

The problem is that we miss the whole point of our existence, the very purpose for which we were created. God made us for the relationship of His perfect love. While we are not capable of perfect performance this side of eternity, we are capable of perfect love. We can settle in our hearts that we will choose God's love and the pursuit of a love relationship with Him above all else, no matter what comes our way.

The day my husband and I made this decision we were in the hospital with our middle daughter, who was six weeks old. She had seemed a perfectly healthy baby until an allergic reaction to the protein in my breast milk landed us in the intensive care unit. The doctors told us on the fourth day of our visit that Ashley needed emergency surgery, and they did not expect her to survive. They gave us five minutes to tell our baby goodbye.

My heart was shattered. I so desperately wanted to scoop her up and run out of the hospital. I wanted to somehow breathe my life into hers. I wanted to take her place. I could handle my own death so much easier than the death of my child. Art prayed over Ashley, we both said our goodbyes, and then, with tears streaming down our faces, we let her go.

When Art took me outside to the hospital parking lot, I collapsed into his arms. He gently cupped my face in his hands and reminded me that Ashley was God's child to give and His to take back. "Lysa, God loves Ashley even more than we do," he gently told me. "We must trust His plan."

Art then asked me to do something, and it changed my whole perspective on my relationship with God. "We have to get it settled in our hearts that we will love God no matter the outcome of Ashley's surgery," he said.

At first I resented Art's desire that we love God in this way. I feared it might give Him the impression it was okay to take Ashley.

With all my being I wanted to hold on to my child and refuse God. Yet, though I was heartbroken, I also felt God's compassion. I felt Him drawing me close and pouring out His tender mercy. God knew firsthand the pain we were feeling because He'd felt it Himself. I knew that, ultimately, I had no ability to control my child's future. With tears pouring from our eyes, Art and I released our sweet Ashley to the Lord and promised to love Him no matter what.

It was as if the more I fell into God's arms, the less the pain of the moment seared my heart. Feeling the power of God took away the fear of the unknown. I stopped thinking about the what-if's and let my soul simply say, *Okay. God, in this minute I choose rest with You. I will not let my mind go to the minutes that are coming. I will simply be in this moment and face it with peace.*

That day we settled our love for God not just for this situation but for all time. Though we did not feel at all happy, a gentle covering of unexplainable joy settled over our hearts. Knowing that the One who loved Ashley even more than we did was taking care of her, and that His plan for her was perfect, brought peace in the middle of heartbreak.

The end of this chapter of Ashley's life was miraculous and wonderful. Though the doctors can't explain how, she made a full recovery. Who can understand why God answers prayer the way He does? We just know we're grateful. And we can also know that no matter God's answer, our hearts were settled to trust and love Him. This kind of radical obedience brings about a depth of relationship with God you can't get any other way.

Nothing in life is certain. Circumstances roll in and out like the ocean's tide. The unknown can sometimes seem so frightening as we ponder all the tragic possibilities that we know can and do happen to people. We catch ourselves wondering what the next page of life might hold. We can't stop or control the things that roll our way any more than we can stop the water's edge. But we can make the minute-by-minute choice to let our souls rest in God.

> Rest knowing all is so safe in My Hands. Rest is Trust. Ceaseless activity is distrust. Without the knowledge that I am working for you, you do not rest. Inaction then would be the outcome of despair. My Hand is not shortened that it cannot save. Know that, repeat it, rely on it, welcome the knowledge, and delight in it. Such a truth is as a hope flung to a drowning man. Every repetition of it is one pull nearer shore and safety. [1]

And with that knowledge safely tucked inside my heart, I can face anything life throws in my direction.

Dear Lord, teach me how to give up the control I try to maintain as I experience uncertainties and hard times. Guide me in pursuing a love relationship with You above all else today. In Jesus' name, amen.

🌿 Reflect and Respond:

How will giving it all to God help you feel more at ease today? Write down three things you are thankful for in the midst of a situation that is less than ideal. Turn these things into a prayer in which you praise God for His goodness.

15

The Power to Obey

---

*Do not love the world or anything in the world.
If anyone loves the world, love for the Father is not
in them. For everything in the world—the lust of
the flesh, the lust of the eyes, and the pride of life—
comes not from the Father but from the world.*

1 John 2:15-16

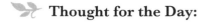 **Thought for the Day:**

It is His power that enables us to do what we're called to do.

THERE'S A BATTLE GOING on today.

The combat isn't always in plain sight. We might not even realize it's going on, but Satan is constantly bombarding us with things to pull us away from what God has called us to do.

But because Christ is the very source of radical obedience, and it is His love that compels us, then it is His power that enables us to do what we're called to do. No amount of pleading from the enemy can overpower God's true will.

Know this: Satan will do everything he can to convince you to say no to God. Satan's very name means "one who separates." He wants to separate you from God's best by offering what seems "very good" from a worldly perspective. He wants you to deny Christ's power in you. He wants to distract you from God's radical purpose for you.

The apostle John warned us of Satan's strategic plan

> Do not love the world or anything in the world. If anyone loves the world, love for the Father is not in them. For everything in the world—the lust of the flesh, the lust of the eyes, and the pride of life—comes not from the Father but from the world (1 John 2:15-16).

The *Life Application Bible* offers this insight

> Some people think that worldliness is limited to external behavior—the people we associate with, the places we go, the activities we enjoy. Worldliness is also internal because it begins in the heart and is characterized by three attitudes: 1. the lust of the flesh—preoccupation with gratifying physical desires; 2. the lust of the eyes—craving and accumulating things, bowing down to the god of materialism; and 3. pride of life—obsession of one's status or importance...By contrast, God values self-control, a spirit of generosity, and a commitment to humble service. It is possible to give the impression of avoiding worldly pleasures while still harboring worldly attitudes in your heart.[1]

It all started way back in paradise with our fruit-loving friend, Eve. She had God's best and traded it all because Satan convinced her that worldly good was more appealing and worth the swap: "When the woman saw that the fruit of the tree was good for food [physical need: the cravings of sinful man] and pleasing to the eye [psychological need: lust of the eyes], and also desirable for gaining wisdom [emotional need: boasting of what he has and does], she took some and ate it [sin separated man from God's best]" (Genesis 3:6). The rest of Genesis 3 covers the shame, hiding, blaming, punishment, and banishment from the Garden.

But, thankfully, this story doesn't end in Genesis 3.

Jesus came and everything changed. He faced temptation just like Eve: "Jesus was led by the Spirit into the wilderness to be tempted by the devil" (Matthew 4:1). And He was tempted in the same three ways that Eve was tempted, only Jesus' temptations were magnified a hundredfold. Eve was in a lush garden with delicious food, an incredible companion, and all the comforts of paradise. Jesus had been in a desert for 40 days, where He went without food, companionship, or comfort of any sort. Satan tempted Him with food that was outside of God's plan for someone who was fasting (physical need: the cravings of sinful man), an opportunity to prove Himself (emotional need: boasting of what he has and does), and the riches of the world (psychological need: lust of the eyes). Jesus withstood the temptations because instead of taking His eyes off of God, He intentionally focused on God and refuted each of Satan's temptations by quoting God's Word.

Satan has no new tricks up his sleeve. He still has nothing better to tempt us with than worldly things. Physical, emotional, and psychological pleasures that fall outside the will of God are still what Satan is using to pull the hearts of God's people away.

For me, the most amazing part of looking at Eve's temptation in relation to Jesus' temptation is what happens next in each of their lives. Eve turns away from God and says yes to worldly distractions. The next chapter of her life is tragic. Eve has two sons, one of whom kills the other. Jesus turns to God and says yes to His divine plan. The next chapter of His life is triumphant. Jesus begins His ministry here on earth.

Something will happen next in our life as well.

Will the next page in your life be filled with doubts and distractions? Or will it be filled with discovering the blessing of answering God's call on your life?

The choice is yours to make.

Dear Lord, I need Your help in the battle to resist Satan's pitfalls. Guide me in my daily decisions so that I can walk in favor through what You have called me to do. In Jesus' name, amen.

🌱 Reflect and Respond:

How has Satan been tempting you to say "no" to God? Set a plan in motion.

1. Identify what things have been major sources of struggle for you.

2. Make an action plan for how to recognize these

temptations when they are occurring and how you will combat them.

3. Put this plan to good use! If you know you will be entering a situation that entertains old habits or temptations, decide beforehand not to engage in that behavior. Instead, remember how you have planned to say yes to God above all else.

16

True Disciples

---

*Simon answered, "Master, we've worked hard
all night and haven't caught anything. But
because you say so, I will let down the nets."*

Luke 5:5

Thought for the Day:

Our calling is revealed as we walk in daily obedience to Christ
in the little things.

JUST BE OBEDIENT TO God. Sounds easy, right? That's before
the rush of the day sets in. Chaos. Frustrations. But in the midst of
your storm, it's important to be intentional about your obedience.

The story of Simon Peter is a New Testament account from the
life of Jesus that shows a true disciple walking in radical obedience
to God.

> He [Jesus] saw at the water's edge two boats, left
> there by the fishermen, who were washing their nets.
> He got into one of the boats, the one belonging to
> Simon, and asked him to put out a little from shore.

> Then he sat down and taught the people from the
> boat. When he had finished speaking, he said to
> Simon, "Put out into deep water, and let down the
> nets for a catch" (Luke 5:2-4).

Did you notice that there were two boats on the shore that day,
and Jesus specifically chose Simon Peter's? Why? Because Jesus knew
Simon Peter had a radically obedient heart and would be willing to
do what He asked him—even when it made no sense.

I like Peter's response to Jesus' request: "Master, we've worked
hard all night and haven't caught anything. But because you say so,
I will let down the nets" (verse 5). Do you hear what Peter is saying?
"Though I'm tired from working all night, though I don't think You
know much about fishing, and though it makes no sense at all in
human terms…because You say so, I will do it."

How many times have I found myself in Peter's position and
not responded in obedience the way he did? It saddens my heart to
remember the occasions I've ignored Jesus' call for my radical obedience because I was tired, or because I didn't really believe Jesus would
work miraculously in a particular situation, or mostly because the
Lord's request made no sense in human terms.

I often wonder now at the blessings I've missed because of my
lack of obedience. Look at what happened to Peter because of his
obedience.

> When they had [let the nets down], they caught such
> a large number of fish that their nets began to break.
> So they signaled their partners in the other boat to
> come and help them, and they came and filled both

boats so full that they began to sink. When Simon
Peter saw this, he fell at Jesus' knees and said, "Go
away from me, Lord; I am a sinful man!" For he and
all his companions were astonished at the catch of
fish they had taken, and so were James and John, the
sons of Zebedee, Simon's partners (Luke 5:6-10).

But Simon Peter's blessing that day didn't end with a huge catch
of fish. His radical obedience to Jesus' simple request ultimately
resulted in him discovering the calling on his life.

James and John, the sons of Zebedee, were surprised
also. They were working together with Simon. Then
Jesus said to Simon, "Do not be afraid. From now on
you will fish for men." When they came to land with
their boats, they left everything and followed Jesus
(Luke 5:10-11 NLV).

We have to remember that Simon Peter didn't know that something as mundane as lowering his net into the water would change
his life—but it did! And that's how it can be for us. Our calling is
revealed as we walk in daily obedience to Christ in the little things.

That's what's remarkable about radical obedience. You don't
know where it will lead. You don't know how God will use it. That's
what I love about Peter's story. It shows us so much about the radically obedient life.

First, our call to obedience may challenge our pride. God hates a
prideful attitude (James 4:6). Many times the little steps leading to
the bigger steps in our calling will be tests that help whittle the pride

out of our heart. Peter, for instance, could have easily questioned Jesus' fishing knowledge...after all, Peter was a professional fisherman and Jesus was a carpenter. But Peter chose to swallow his pride and take the small step of obedience.

Second, our experiences equip us for our calling. God doesn't waste our experiences in life. I know in my own life God has been able to weave everything together to form a beautiful tapestry of good experiences, bad experiences, hurtful things, joyous things, professional jobs, ministry jobs, and everything else to prepare me for the work He is in the process of revealing to me. The same was true for Simon Peter. Yesterday he was fishing for fish; today he would be fishing for men.

Third, our obedience may inspire others to respond. What a radical blessing! As we respond in obedience, others will catch the vision and respond to God's calling on their own lives. Think of it. It wasn't just Peter's life that changed that day. The lives of his fishing partners, James and John, were never the same either. And it started with Peter saying yes to Jesus.

A word of caution at this point. We need to be careful not to fall into the trap of thinking that our blessings for radical obedience will profit our accounts and fill our pockets. Yes, Peter got a boatload of fish as a result of his obedience, but notice what he did: "So they pulled their boats up on shore, left everything and followed him" (Luke 5:11).

They didn't celebrate their banner fishing day.

They didn't consider the fish a just reward for all their hard work.

They didn't sell the fish and use the money to buy more boats and hang out a new shingle announcing their expanded fishing fleet.

No, they were only thinking of the person who allowed it to happen—and they left it all behind to follow Him.

Now, I'm no fishing expert, but leaving behind all the equipment needed to support your livelihood seems pretty radical. Sometimes God will ask us to abandon our comfort zones, the things we rely on most, and the materials we think we need in order to survive. God wants to build our reliance upon Him and bless us in ways we can't even begin to imagine.

So here's your challenge: Anchor the ship, cast your nets aside, and follow the One who cares for you.

Dear Lord, thank You for speaking to me today about radical obedience. Use this teaching to grow my dependence on You and Your plans for my life. In Jesus' name, amen.

🌿 Reflect and Respond:

Are you struggling to respond in obedience in an area of your life? Identify what you are having a hard time being obedient with. Reflect on the three points above in relation to your struggle.

17

The Floodgates of Blessing

*"Bring the whole tithe into the storehouse, that there may be
food in my house. Test me in this," says the LORD Almighty,
"and see if I will not throw open the floodgates
of heaven and pour out so much blessing that
there will not be room enough to store it."*

MALACHI 3:10

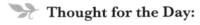 **Thought for the Day:**

God wants us to venture into truly abundant giving.

TRUST. ISN'T THAT WHY more of us don't offer all we have to
God? We don't trust that He really will throw open the floodgates
of blessing in return.

Sacrificial giving is one of the few times God asks us to test Him.

Yet for many years I found myself unwilling to accept the challenge. I was willing to tithe, but not willing to go beyond what I
felt comfortable giving. Outside our comfort zone, however, is the
very place God calls us to. He wants us to venture into truly abundant giving. He wants us to get out from under our own selfishness
with our possessions and accept His invitation to become radically

obedient with what we own. Then, not only will He bless us, but He will lavish blessing upon blessing on us.

I saw this firsthand when I was saving money for a new outfit.

I started this "new outfit fund" because of an embarrassing situation I found myself in during a country club speaking engagement. I was wearing what I thought was a very nice outfit. When I showed up at the event, however, I quickly realized that not only was my outfit a little out of style, but my white discount store shoes were the only light-colored foot apparel in the entire building. (Not being a queen of fashion, I was unaware of the rule that white shoes have to wait until after Memorial Day in some parts of the country.) Everyone had on dark-colored shoes, so with every step I took, I felt as though my feet were screaming, "White shoes! Everyone look at my shocking white shoes!"

You'll be happy to know that not even white shoes could stop me from sharing about Jesus with this lovely group of women, but you'd better believe I was determined to update and improve my wardrobe.

It took me a while, but when I managed to save up one hundred dollars in my fund, I set a date to go shopping with some of my fashion-savvy friends.

Just a few days before I was to go shopping, another dear friend phoned to ask me to pray for her family's financial situation. They could not make ends meet and had many bills they were unable to pay. She mentioned they needed one hundred dollars immediately. While she was only asking me to pray for her and nothing more, I knew God was looking for a response from me that would honor Him. I prayed for my friend and I obeyed God's prompting to give to her the money I'd saved.

The day arrived for my shopping trip, and I must admit that

instead of being excited, I felt a pang of dread. I knew that because I had given my money away, I could only look and not purchase anything. I didn't want my fashion friends to think I was wasting their time, so I decided I would put whatever clothes they picked out for me on hold and pray that God would provide the means to return later and purchase them.

While I was moping about and strategizing, God was at work in my friends' hearts. After trying on three beautiful outfits complete with shoes and accessories, I returned to my dressing room to try and decide which outfit to put on hold. While I dressed, my friends took everything to the checkout counter and treated me to a $700 shopping spree!

That afternoon, I experienced the amazing truth of today's verse: "Test me in this," says the LORD Almighty, "and see if I will not throw open the floodgates of heaven and pour out so much blessing that there will not be room enough to store it" (Malachi 3:10). I was shocked and humbled that God had taken the little gift I'd given to my friend and returned it sevenfold through other friends.

God owns it all. We are simply managers of His resources. When we pursue the beautiful opportunities of sacrificial living, we freely acknowledge that truth and then reap the blessings. When we come to understand that we're giving up what was never ours to begin with, we're walking in radical obedience.

Dear Lord, I give thanks and praise to You today for all of the blessings You've poured into my life. Help me to be a sacrificial giver with a heart to serve others, God, so that I may further Your kingdom. In Jesus' name, amen.

🍃 Reflect and Respond:

Have you been living a life of sacrificial giving? Whether you have or have not, let God speak to you about it today. Take some time to be in constant prayer about what you can do to improve upon this area in your spiritual life.

18

The Mother Load

These commandments that I give you today
are to be on your hearts. Impress them on your children.
Talk about them when you sit at home and when you walk
along the road, when you lie down and when you get up.

DEUTERONOMY 6:6-7

Thought for the Day:

My kids were never meant to carry the weight of a mama's need for validation.

WE MOMS SHOULD NEVER build the stability of our identity on the fragile choices of our kids.

Let me say it again just so this crucial truth can sink in a little deeper. I'm repeating it for no other reason, sweet sister, than the fact that I need this message. So, forgive me if this devotion preaches a message only to myself.

We moms should never build the stability of our identity on the fragile choices of our kids.

I have five amazing kids. I really do. They are wildly funny, imaginative, moody, opinionated, strong, weak, happy, sad, good, and sometimes not so good. In other words, they are pretty normal. And while I've done everything in my power to raise them to turn out amazingly awesome—and they very well might turn out amazingly awesome—there aren't any guarantees.

Sometimes bad parents raise terrific kids.

And sometimes terrific parents raise kids that chase bad things their whole life.

So what's a mama to do?

Embrace the process. Learn from the process. Let God speak to us during the process. And see the process of raising kids as an ongoing opportunity to invest beyond ourselves.

It's a wonderful opportunity to show them what a life of being obedient to the Lord looks like. It's something we should be excited about. There are so many ways we get to build upon our strong foundation in Christ as mothers.

We get to love our kids like crazy. Pray for them faithfully. Talk to them regularly. Listen to them tenderly. Model honesty and integrity. And point them to Jesus at every turn.

We get to do all that.

Tucked within these privileges is the reward. As long as I look for the reward within the process, I won't misplace my expectations. I have to rest in the assurance that God sees everything I invest in these kids. And He will use every step of this process for good. Good for me and somehow good for them. It will be good. But this process won't always make me feel good or look good.

If I always expect my kids to make me feel good or look good, I am setting us all up for failure. My kids were never meant to carry the weight of a mama's need for validation. I can't let their failures send me to bed. And I can't wear their successes like mommy medals of honor.

Motherhood is tough, you know? It really is.

However, it's also our only opportunity to reach into the generations to come and make a difference. So, an imperfect but wonderful difference I will make.

Like Nelson Mandela once expressed in an interview, "I never was a saint. I'm just a sinner who keeps on trying."

Isn't that a great description of all us mamas? Keep trying. Keep going. Keep saying yes to God. He sees all you do. He can help you embrace this process of investing wisely in your kids. And He will hold your identity in the certainty of His love…no matter what choices your kids make.

Dear Lord, thank You for my children. I know I am not always as thankful as I should be. Help me to see the process of raising them as a daily privilege. In Jesus' name, amen.

🌿 Reflect and Respond:

Do you struggle with owning your children's successes and failures? As an exercise, choose a fellow mom friend who you know could use some encouragement right now. Take a few minutes to write a letter, make a phone call, send a text, or write an email.

19

I Want to Run Away

---

*If you carefully observe all these commands
I am giving you to follow—to love the LORD your God,
to walk in obedience to him and to hold fast to him—
then the LORD will drive out all these nations before you,
and you will dispossess nations larger and stronger than you.*

DEUTERONOMY 11:22-23

Thought for the Day:

All that God ever wants from me is to want Him. Love Him. Acknowledge Him.

TO ME, ONE OF the worst feelings in the world is feeling stuck.

Stuck in a situation where I can't see things getting better. I look at the next five minutes, five hours, five days—and all I see are the same hard patterns being repeated over and over and over.

I try to give myself a little pep rally of sorts and tap into that Pollyanna girl that's inside me somewhere. It's the part of me that knows the glass is half full and chooses to see the bright side.

But Pollyanna can't be found.

Life suddenly feels as though it will forever be this way.

And a dark funk eclipses me.

This happened to me when my two oldest daughters were babies. Hope was not quite 16 months old when I gave birth to Ashley. I was thankful for these two amazing gifts. I knew they were blessings. I loved them very much.

But there was this other side of motherhood no one talked to me about beforehand. It never came up at my baby shower or a doctor's appointment or in conversations with other mommies.

In the midst of all the pink happiness, the dark funk came—this desperate feeling that life would forever be an endless string of sleepless nights. Leaky diapers. Needy cries.

Forever.

One night in between feedings I went out to get some baby Tylenol. I pulled into a parking space right in front of the restaurant beside the drugstore and stared inside. Normal people were in there. Laughing. Eating. Having fun conversations. They had on cute outfits and fixed hairdos.

I looked at my reflection in the rearview mirror and I cried, thinking, *This is my life. Forever.*

Suddenly I had this crazy desire to run away. Far away.

And then guilt slammed into my already fragile heart, and I convinced myself God was going to punish me for feeling this way and take one of my babies. Teach me a lesson. Smite me for being so stinkin' selfish.

I cried until I could barely breathe.

I thought about this recently when I started feeling stuck in a different situation that seemed so big and made me so sad. I felt myself on the edge of that dark funk thinking, *This is the way it's going to be forever.*

But then I remembered that night I was crying in my car. Those days of diapers and no sleep weren't forever. It was a season that came and went. And this would play out that way too.

It's the rhythm of life. The ebb and flow of struggles and victories.

Sometimes all I need to do is close my eyes and whisper, "Are You here, God? Hold me. Breathe courage into my weak will. Help me."

And in that moment I realize that all God ever wants from me is to want Him. Love Him. Acknowledge Him.

In the midst of my struggles. In the midst of my victories. "God, I love You. I don't love this situation, but I love You. Therefore, I have everything I need to keep putting one foot in front of the other and walk through until I get to the other side of this."

One step at a time. With the full assurance God is okay with me even when I'm not okay with me.

"If you carefully observe all these commands I am giving you to follow—to love the LORD your God, to walk in obedience to him and to hold fast to him—then the LORD will drive out all these nations before you, and you will dispossess nations larger and stronger than you" (Deuteronomy 11:22-23).

I love how the Scriptures say "hold fast" to the Lord, telling us to cling tightly to God. However, the dark funk causes me to "hold slow." That's when I hold loosely, maybe even reluctantly, to God. To make Him the last thing I try when I'm stumbling and falling. But if I close my eyes and simply whisper, "God…" at the utterance of His name He "dispossesses" things trying to possess me.

Then I can see this is a season. This isn't how it's going to be forever. Though my circumstances may not change today, my outlook surely can. And if my mind can rise above, my heart gets unstuck.

Dear Lord, You are so loving and good. Help me to see my situation with clear perspective and know You are on my side helping me through what seems to be impossible. I know with Your help, all things are possible. In Jesus' name, amen.

❧ Reflect and Respond:

Do you feel stuck in a situation right now? Choose to hold on to God as you go through this challenging time. Pray honest prayers and be sure to take time to listen. Though God may not deliver you out of the current season you are in, He will surely give you the strength to get through it.

20

The Cussing Thoughts

Let us hold unswervingly to the hope we profess,
for he who promised is faithful.

Hebrews 10:23

🌿 Thought for the Day:

God has called me a child of God, but I have to choose to live this legacy.

THE SKY WAS BLUE. The snow crisp white. The mountain slopes full of choices to be made. Which run will we take?

A "blue run" is what we tackled first. This is how slopes are labeled by the ski officials. The officials whose job it is to inform skiers exactly what they are about to get into. Yes, those of us crazy enough to strap slick, glorified Popsicle sticks to our feet and careen down a mountain need to be informed.

Green for beginners. Blue for intermediates. Black for the advanced and those who think they are advanced until they get too far to turn back. Bummer.

No, we would be smart with this skiing thing. We wouldn't

overestimate our abilities. We wouldn't be tackling the black runs. But blue? Yes, please.

So blue it was. The sky and the run. It was the perfect skiing adventure.

Until…the moguls.

We'd been on several lovely runs down the same slope when Art suggested we try a different lift taking us to a different slope. Huh? I am emotionally allergic to different. I like to discover something that's good and stick with it. Why mess with what's working? With what feels good?

Um, no thanks.

"It will be great," he insisted as he headed on over to the new lift.

Either I was going to follow him or be left behind. He was going. That's when I had my first not-so-nice thought. I call them cussing thoughts. It's not that I was actually saying cuss words. No, more like really negative thoughts I wouldn't want to broadcast out loud. You know what I mean?

So a new slope it would be.

Things started out well. Then the slope got a little interesting. Have you ever heard people say something like, "Everything was going fine until we hit a little bump in the road"? Well, try a steep mountain full of nothing but bumps. Like the kind that could careen you off the side of the mountain. Or snap your legs in half.

As fear coursed through every fiber of my body, my mind filled up with all things negative and derogatory.

What's so ironic is just an hour before I was helping my friend Laci learn to ski. She was terrified, but I was completely confident. "You can do this," I assured her. "Don't look down the mountain and think you can't get through this. Look across the mountain. Just ski from side to side on the slopes, and before you know it you'll be safely at the bottom."

I hadn't really taught Laci how to ski. I'd taught her how to think. And when she got into the right mental mode, she learned to ski. She had to resist the cussing thoughts so she could choose the corrected thoughts. Because dark thoughts are like a black run down the mountain—once you get on the black slope of cussing thoughts, they will take you down to places you don't want to go.

Now it was my turn to apply my own advice. And I failed miserably. I made that run so much more difficult by letting the cussing thoughts come in and bring me down.

How like life.

Every day we're going to hit bumpy spots in life. Someone will do something that rubs you wrong. Cussing thoughts or corrected thoughts? You don't get that opportunity you felt you deserved. Cussing thoughts or corrected thoughts?

A cussing thought can become a corrected thought by asking three questions.

1. Is this thought in line with truth?
2. Is this thought in line with who I am?
3. Is this thought in line with who I want to be?

God has taught me how to think using His truth, but I have to make the choice to apply what I've learned. God has called me a child of God, but I have to choose to live this legacy. God has challenged me to live out Hebrews 10:23, "Let us hold unswervingly to the hope we profess, for he who promised is faithful."

"Hold unswervingly." Hold. Unswervingly. What does this mean?

God has challenged me to grow in my knowledge of Him, but I have to choose whether or not to display this growth through my actions. My words. My decision to be obedient to Him.

Think according to the truth. Live according to the truth. Then His hope will be displayed in my life.

Just as mountain slopes have options for which runs to take… so do I with the thoughts I think. Cussing thoughts or corrected thoughts are my choice.

Dear Lord, I am so grateful for Your truth. Give me strength today as I hit some bumpy spots in my journey of obedience. Make my thoughts pure and in alignment with Your Word. In Jesus' name, amen.

🌿 Reflect and Respond:

What cussing thoughts are you having today?

Write down one in particular you're struggling with. Then write down a truth-based thought to replace it with.

21

Sitting at Home, Alone

*In Him all the fullness of Deity dwells in bodily form,
and in Him you have been made complete,
and He is the head over all rule and authority.*

COLOSSIANS 2:9-10 NASB

Thought for the Day:

Don't put the whole of your identity into the smallness of a situation.

THEY WERE LAUGHING IN their matching neon-pink T-shirts with the words "Bethany's Birthday Girls" printed on the front. They were going bowling after school. Then to get pizza. Then to a sleepover.

When Bethany passed out the shirts that morning, I pretended to be too busy to notice. I stayed hyper focused on unpacking my book bag and placing its contents into my locker. And then I hurried off to my first class. It was clear. Bethany had made a list of her friends and I hadn't been included. I thought I would be. We'd gotten together before. I'd invited her to my pool party.

"No big deal," I tried to tell myself all day. I had plans that night too. To sit at home—alone—and wonder why I hadn't been chosen.

It's been years since I watched those neon-pink shirts all pile into a station wagon after school and drive away, but it hasn't been years since I've heard the negative inside chatter that ensued afterward.

"You're not liked."

"You weren't invited."

"You weren't chosen."

When we continue to let such destructive words fall hard on our souls, they don't leave any room for the truth to flourish. Lies are what reign in the absence of truth. It's a chance for the enemy to reach us at our core.

What seem to be simple thoughts are actually very dangerous weapons Satan uses to break down our relationships, emotional state, and our walk with the Lord.

Scary stuff.

But here's what I wish I could have told my little sans-pink-shirt-self back then, and what I need to remember when those same feelings creep in today: Don't put the whole of your identity into the smallness of this situation.

I wasn't invited to Bethany's party. And that stunk.

Not getting a pink T-shirt that day felt like a defining moment, but it wasn't a moment that defined my identity.

It was a moment. And moments shift. People are fickle. People shift.

You might be feeling that negative self-chatter is holding you captive. It's easy to be swallowed up by the intensity of a moment. But since we're working together as women who say yes to God, we must make a commitment to say no to that inner dialogue. When we fill ourselves with His Word, Spirit, and the truth about where our identity lies, we can stand firmly in who He says we are. Not anyone else.

In the moment Bethany made the list of who to invite to her party, I wasn't on the top of her mind. Not because she didn't like me, but simply because she hadn't thought about it.

It was a small situation. And I can't put the whole of my identity into the smallness of this situation or any other, for that matter.

Our verse of the day echoes this idea. "In Him all the fullness of Deity dwells in bodily form, and in Him you have been *made complete*, and He is the head over all rule and authority" (Colossians 2:9-10 NASB, emphasis added).

I have been made complete. I am filled up by Christ with acceptance, with love. The completeness and fullness of my identity in Him can't be shaken. I can place the wholeness of my identity in that reality. And I can see everything else as small in comparison.

Dear Lord, I want to be a woman who says yes to You instead of feeling held captive by the negative thoughts Satan plants in my mind. Your acceptance and love make me complete. I don't need anyone or anything else to make me whole. In Jesus' name, amen.

Reflect and Respond:

Are you still processing a past hurt that seemed like a defining moment in your life?

Reflect on our verse of the day and spend some time in prayer. Consider talking about your hurts with a trusted friend, family member, or pastor who can offer godly counsel.

22

From Overpowered to Empowered

*He said to me, "My grace is sufficient for you,
for my power is made perfect in weakness."
Therefore I will boast all the more gladly about my weaknesses,
so that Christ's power may rest on me.*

2 CORINTHIANS 12:9

Thought for the Day:

The fact that I have weaknesses doesn't make everything about me weak.

IT WAS ONE OF those days. I was driving to the airport in the pouring rain. The skies were gray. The day felt a bit gloomy. And so did I. A lot of little things were swarming my thoughts. Feelings of inadequacy were stinging. "There are so many things I'm responsible for, and I never have enough hours in the day. I do enough to keep things from sinking, but I wonder if I'm doing anything well. I don't think I am…"

The more I focused on these thoughts, the more overpowered I became. The more overpowered I became, the more withdrawn I felt.

I pulled into the parking space and started to fight with my luggage. My suitcase has two wheels missing. And of course I keep intending to do something about this, but I don't have time. So I make do with a crazy suitcase and a crazy life and a crazy sense I should pack up my family and move out west somewhere. We should live on a ranch where we grow our own food and I cook beans in a black pot over an open flame.

Surely that would fix everything.

Except that I know it wouldn't because the chaos isn't from my circumstances—it's inside me.

I boarded the plane. I stared out the window. I watched the gray clouds envelop us. And then the gray broke. Suddenly, we rose above the clouds and the sun was shining brightly. The sky was fabulously clear.

The clouds were just a temporary covering. They didn't stop the sun from shining. They just prevented my eyes from seeing the sun. And it wasn't just the sky that emerged a little brighter. My mood did as well.

I started to shift from feeling overpowered to empowered as I realized three things.

1. *Just because I feel it doesn't make it real.* Just like I felt the sun was gone but it wasn't, I might feel that I'm not doing anything well, but it doesn't make it true. The fact that I have weaknesses doesn't make everything about me weak. I have plenty of strengths. All I have to do is ask a couple of my friends or my family members to help me see what I do well. I can celebrate those and then get a plan for bettering things that need

improvement. I can start by identifying one thing to improve on this month, and then do a little toward making that one thing better.

2. A *lot of people would trade their best day for my worst day.* Yes, I have a lot to manage. And yes, sometimes things get a little foggy. But that doesn't mean I have to stay swallowed up in the gray. That means I need to get my head above the clouds and see all the many places where the sun is shining brightly in my life. Then I can start making a list of things for which I am thankful.

3. My *mind needs some space to think.* If I always run at a breakneck pace, I'm eventually going to break. My mind is a powerful tool, capable of seeing things that can be done more efficiently and effectively if I give myself time to think. When is the last time I just sat quietly with a pen and paper and asked the Lord to help me think?

As 2 Corinthians 12:9 teaches, God's power is made perfect in weakness. When I'm sinking in thoughts of inadequacy and plans to relocate out west, I remember that my ability is not based on what I can do. My ability and strength come from the One who can do all things. When the Lord works in me and through my weaknesses, I feel the transformation from being overpowered to empowered taking place.

If the clouds have been looming close lately, maybe it's time to stop. Pause. Lift your eyes to an altitude that can rearrange your attitude.

In this journey there may be days, weeks, or seasons when you feel overwhelmed and overpowered. It is always important to remember to take time to rearrange your perspective.

Dear Lord, only You can provide all I need to stay the course. Please help me as I have days that feel as though the weight of the world is on my shoulders. Help me refocus my attention to You. In Jesus' name, amen.

🌿 Reflect and Respond:

Commit ten minutes, today, to sit quietly with a pen and paper and ask the Lord to help you think. Make a list of five things you are thankful for.

1.

2.

3.

4.

5.

23

Where Faith Gets Awfully Messy

---

*Faith is confidence in what we hope for
and assurance about what we do not see.*

HEBREWS 11:1

🌿 **Thought for the Day:**

Even small faith is completely able to hold you.

IN THE SPRING OF 2012 I had emergency surgery on my ears. And while the pain went away, there is still a really loud, constant ringing in my left ear. Because of this ringing, I've had many sleepless nights, but one night in particular proved to be more than I thought I could handle. The screeching in my ear reached an all-time high, and even the medication didn't help. My throat tightened as frustration of this situation threatened to spill out in a million tears. I could feel myself slipping over a terrifying edge...that edge where hopelessness steps into the moment and you feel too weak to resist it.

I whispered, "I'm slipping, God. I can't stand this another minute. Much less five more minutes. Or five more hours. Seriously, God, I can't. I'm trying to be brave. I've begged for Your healing. And I truly believe You are healing me, but I'm freaking out. And I'm so sorry if 'freaking' is a bad word—I'm still on the fence about that one. But, God, I feel myself falling and I can't figure out what to grab on to."

This is where faith gets awfully messy, isn't it?

Faith.

Most days, I'm like a little kid on the swing going higher and higher without fear. I know the swing will hold me. I know the chains are secure. I'm bold. Assured. Confident.

That night, though, I was terrified of the swing. The chains felt more like unraveling threads with a screaming me dangling at the end. My faith felt small.

But my faith was right in front of me. And when one falls, out of instinct they grab on to whatever is right in front of them.

I want you to know that even small faith is completely able to hold you. It held me that night. Through the minutes and hours I didn't think I could press on.

I started recounting all the ways God made sure my faith was front and center for this slip. I thought about the ways I'd seen His hand even in the previous days.

Recounting His faithfulness secured the chains, showed me I wasn't dangling by a thread out on my own. One helpful discovery was that my husband's sound machine is a gift. That crazy sound machine has aggravated the stink out of me for years, but when I put on the rain setting, it helps soothe the screeching in my ear.

Without having told my pastor about my ear, he sent me a text saying he was praying for me, and God had put 1 Kings 18:41-46 on his heart.

And what are those verses about?

Rain. The sound of a heavy rain.

A rain that happens in between two vastly different displays of faith in Elijah's life. One minute he's swinging with great faith so bold and secure he calls fire down from heaven. Then only a few verses later he's dangling by a thread as he runs and hides in a cave.

The Lord comes to Elijah in a gentle whisper and shows him what to do at the end of that thread. "Go back the way you came" (1 Kings 19:15).

God was saying, "Backtrack and remember all the places I've been faithful in your life. And know with assurance. And boldness. And confidence. I AM. I AM the same faithful God."

Sometimes saying yes to God doesn't mean making a big move. Sometimes it means staying right where we are, knowing God is in control of a seemingly out-of-control situation.

So I let these words slip into my soul. I turn up the sound of rain. I grab on to my faith right in front of me. And I discover I am held by the great I AM. I guess I just wanted to be that friend today who reminds you, no matter what you're going through—the same is true for you.

Dear Lord, thank You for being so faithful, even when it feels as though things are slipping away. Help me today as I let Your promises and truth sink deep into my heart. I know it only takes faith the size of a mustard seed, and sometimes it feels as if that is all I have. Teach me to trust You no matter what the circumstance. In Jesus' name, amen.

🌿 Reflect and Respond:

It is so important that we remember God's faithfulness. It can carry us through those dark times in our lives. Write down three specific situations when the Lord has proven faithful even when you felt hopeless.

1.
2.
3.

24

The Choice to Worry or Worship

*Don't you know that when you offer yourselves to someone
as obedient slaves, you are slaves of the one you obey—
whether you are slaves to sin, which leads to death,
or to obedience, which leads to righteousness?*

ROMANS 6:16

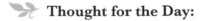 **Thought for the Day:**

When we worship in these hard places, we are reminded that
none of this is about us—it's all about God.

PURSUING OBEDIENCE AND SAYING yes to God has been the
most fulfilling adventure I have ever let my heart follow after. However, the journey has not been without bumps and bruises.

I would be remiss in this teaching of what keeps us from radical
obedience if I did not talk about the great dance between the desire
of our flesh and the desire of God's Spirit in us.

Our flesh seeks the approval of others, is swayed by Satan's voice
of condemnation, and looks for the comfortable way out. God's
Spirit in us opposes Satan and the world's way and offers an unexplainable peace that transcends the circumstances around us.

The dance plays out in my head. There is the pull between condemnation and conviction. If I'm hearing thoughts of condemnation, these only come from Satan. There is no condemnation from Jesus, only conviction. It's important for us to know the difference. Condemnation leaves us feeling hopeless and worthless. Conviction invites us to make positive changes in our lives.

I also sometimes find myself getting caught up in my own weariness and grumbling over the empty places of my life. These are all the places that chip away at my contentment, that nag me into thinking I'm being cheated out of something somehow.

A few years ago, we did a renovation on the house. Things were new and perfect for a couple of days, but it didn't take long with five kids and a dog for the carpet to get stained and the woodwork to get scratched. My car has dings on each of the front doors and a scratch on the driver's side door, and sometimes this bothers me. (We won't even talk about what the inside of my kid-toting vehicle looks like!) With all of their great qualities, my kids sometimes pout, complain, and whine, and this bothers me. My husband and I are crazy about each other but still find ways to get on each other's nerves at times, and this bothers me. I struggle with trying to cram too much into too little time and often find myself running late—which really bothers me. When these little things get piled on top of bigger things, I can really get down.

There are things in my life, little and big, that fall short, don't meet my expectations, and cause grumpy feelings inside my heart. Do you ever sense empty places in your life too?

Usually this happens to me when the busyness of life has crowded out my quiet times with Jesus. When I have not spent enough time allowing the Lord to refuel and refill me, I forget this is not my real home. When my soul gets down, these places can be distracting and difficult. And sometimes the reality is we feel hurt and discouraged.

When we find ourselves in these hard places, we make the choice to worry or worship.

When we worry, we feel we have to come up with justifications and careful explanations for the naysayers. When we worry, we listen to the voices of Acceptance and Rejection. When we worry, we lay awake at night and ponder Satan's lies. When we worry, we have pity parties where the guests of honor are Negative Thinking, Doubt, and Resignation.

But we can make the choice to worship.

When we worship in these hard places, we are reminded that none of this is about us—it's all about God. We turn our focus off of ourselves and back onto God Almighty. God can use the empty places in your life to draw your heart to Him. He is the great love of your life who will never disappoint. He is building your eternal home that will never get broken, dirty, or need redecorating. He is preparing a place of eternal perfect fellowship where no one will be a naysayer. And heaven won't be limited to human time frames, so no one will ever be late…not even me!

Our hearts were made for perfection in the Garden of Eden, but the minute sin came into the picture, strokes of imperfection began to cast a dingy hue. When we know Christ, however, we know this is not all there is. Realizing that this life is temporary helps me to live beyond this moment and rejoice in what is to come. Each time I feel my heart being pulled down into the pit of ungratefulness and grumbling, I recognize it as a call to draw near to the Lord. I thank

Him for the empty places, for they remind me that only He has the ability to fill me completely. In my worship of Him, my soul is safe and comforted and reassured and at peace.

We all worship something. We must choose whom—or what—we will worship. Will it be the opinions of others, our fears, or even our own comfort? Or will it be the One who created our souls to worship? Whatever we worship, we will obey. As we choose to be radically obedient and say yes to the Lord, we must be radical about choosing to worship Him and Him alone.

Dear Lord, may You be the only thing I worship. I want to be so wrapped up in my relationship with You that I forget about my worries and worldly desires. Remind me of this today, God. In Jesus' name, amen.

❧ Reflect and Respond:

What are you worshipping today?

If something is taking precedence over your devotion to the Lord, take note of it. Start with small steps in placing God at the center of your world.

25

When My Wild Heart Pushes the Boundary

Those who trust in themselves are fools,
but those who walk in wisdom are kept safe.

PROVERBS 28:26

Thought for the Day:

God's instructions and boundaries are protective restrictions meant to define where safe freedom can be found.

"MRS. TERKEURST, YOUR DOG ran away to our house... AGAIN."

"Mrs. TerKeurst, I think I might have just seen your dog running down the street."

"Mrs. TerKeurst, this is one of your neighbors just letting you know we're about to drop off your dog we saw running around our neighborhood."

"Mrs. TerKeurst, this is the animal clinic. I believe we have your dog."

"Mrs. TerKeurst, do you own two dogs?"

Actually, I own three dogs. But my two outside dogs, Champ and Chelsea, are sometimes delinquent dogs. I love them. They love me. But they love running away more.

I can't tell you the number of sleepless nights I've spent fretting over my dogs. Several times we've enlisted our friends to pray for Champ and Chelsea. However, this sort of backfired on us once. One of our friends knew Champ had gone missing and miraculously found him in someone's yard miles from our home. He was amazed Champ had run so far. He pulled into the driveway, coaxed Champ into his car, and called me with breathless excitement to announce he'd found my beloved dog.

But five minutes before my friend got to my house, Champ returned home. When my friend pulled into my driveway carrying a Champ look-alike, we both about fell over. He had just kidnapped someone else's dog—right from their front yard!

Oh my glory be.

It was time to do something.

I used to think invisible fences were cruel. Because I couldn't stand the thought of my dog getting a shock, I looked into getting a regular fence. But we live on 12 acres of land, and installing a regular fence was simply out of the question.

So an invisible fence it would have to be. After all, a shock to keep them inside the safe boundary is a lot better than what might happen outside the boundary.

Boundaries aren't cruel barriers meant to keep my dogs from freedom. They are protective restrictions meant to define where safe freedom can be found. And my dogs aren't the only ones who need to remember this lesson. I need to remember this and apply it to the protective restrictions God has for me.

Why? Because there's usually some sort of boundary my wild heart tries to push against. Have you ever found yourself rationalizing some situation in your life where you know you aren't doing what God said we should do? *Does God really want us to love our enemy? Is it really important to not let the sun go down on my anger? Do I really need to pray and read my Bible every day? Oh, grumbling isn't so bad…I mean, everyone finds something to complain about.*

I push against the boundary. Sometimes I even break through it. But what's waiting on the other side isn't freedom.

We will never find freedom if we remain stubborn in our own wants and desires without seeking discernment from the Lord. Rationalizing thoughts and actions of the flesh and ignoring God's whispers is an act of disobedience. One that moves us farther and farther away from the safety of His will.

Oh Lord, let my wild heart always remember…Your instructions, Your boundaries, aren't cruel barriers to keep me from freedom. They are protective restrictions meant to define where safe freedom can be found.

And, Lord, if You can teach this same lesson to my dogs, my neighbors and I would be ever so grateful.

> *Dear Lord, thank You for the protective hand You have placed over me. Cultivate in me an obedient heart that seeks to live in the safe freedom of Your boundaries. In Jesus' name, amen.*

❧ Reflect and Respond:

What is one thing that God has been asking you to surrender to Him?

We know that any need we try to meet outside of God's perfect will is a step into a danger zone. Spend some time reflecting on the verse of the day as you surrender an issue to God you have been rationalizing.

26

The Rip Current of People Pleasing

You were once darkness,
but now you are light in the Lord.
Live as children of light (for the fruit of the light
consists in all goodness, righteousness and truth)
and find out what pleases the Lord.

EPHESIANS 5:8-10

🌿 Thought for the Day:

Wherever we focus our attention the most, that will become the driving force in our lives.

BRING THE TOPIC OF people pleasing up in a group of women, and the responses are interesting. Most quickly say they struggle with this to some degree. Those who say they don't struggle with people pleasing eventually admit it is present in at least one of their relationships before the conversation is over.

People pleasing is something that affects most of us. And it is something we seem resigned to have to deal with rather than determined to overcome.

Why is that?

One day I tweeted, "Dead giveaway I'm in the rip current of people pleasing—when I dread saying yes but feel powerless to say no."

We all want to be liked. There's nothing wrong with that. But as we travel the path toward love and acceptance, let's take a look at two of the possible motivations behind people pleasing.

Give to Give

One motivation is to give love out of the kindness of our heart. In giving love we feel love. That's good.

Give to Get

Another motivation is to give out of what we hope to get in return. We feel desperate to do more to get more. That's dangerous. It's this second way that gets us into trouble with people pleasing.

It's not wrong to want to make others feel loved, happy, and pleased, but if we are doing it with the motivation of getting things in return, we will set ourselves up for trouble.

Being in constant pursuit of trying to get love by doing more and more will lead to exhaustion. Exhaustion for the giver. Exhaustion for the taker. Exhaustion in the relationship altogether.

Ephesians 5:8-10 says, "You were once darkness, but now you are light in the Lord. Live as children of light (for the fruit of the light consists in all goodness, righteousness and truth) and find out what pleases the Lord."

I like the explanation of what the fruit or evidence is when we walk as children of light—doing what is good, right, and true—as we discern what is pleasing to the Lord.

I am challenged to make this a filter for the decisions I'm making today.

If I'm seeking to please the Lord, I will ask some questions before agreeing to do something for another person. Am I doing this with good motives, right intentions, and true expectations?

Or am I doing this with

Fearful motives—"They might not like me if I say no."

Skewed intentions—"If I do this for them, will they be more likely to do that for me?"

Unrealistic expectations—"I just know if I give a little more, they'll affirm me and I'm desperate for their affirmation."

Whatever we focus most of our attention on will become the driving force in our lives. The more I focus on trying to figure out how to please people, the more of a magnified force people pleasing will become in my life. The more I focus on trying to figure out how to please God, the more of a magnified force He will become in my life.

My focus. My choice.

Dear Lord, help me to break away from my people pleasing tendencies. Guide me in my daily decisions as I battle fearful motives, skewed intentions, and unrealistic expectations. I want to make You the focus, Father, so that You continue to become the magnified force in my life. In Jesus' name, amen.

Reflect and Respond:

Have you experienced the cycle of doing more to get more? Search your heart and ask yourself

- What are my motives?
- Am I seeking to please people or God in this situation?

You may need to place healthy boundaries in your relationships with others so that you can learn when to say yes and when to say no.

27

I'm Going to Disappoint Someone

*On the contrary, we speak as those approved by God
to be entrusted with the gospel.
We are not trying to please people
but God, who tests our hearts.*

1 Thessalonians 2:4

Thought for the Day:

Real love pursues authenticity rather than chasing acceptance.

"Hello, my name is Lysa, and I want people to like me. So I will say yes sometimes when I really want to say no. And when I do say no, I will worry about how much I'm disappointing others."

I would much rather write this in past tense. "I used to struggle with this, but I've really matured past it all. So let me share how I bravely say no and never fret over that decision."

But this isn't a past tense issue in my life.

And no matter how I want to spin what this is, I have to call it people pleasing. Yesterday we talked about the rip current of people pleasing. Today, let's make peace with the fact we're going to disappoint some people as we seek to please God.

It's part of my DNA to love others and avoid disappointing them, but I have to understand that real love is honest. Real love cares enough about other people to say no when saying yes would build up a barrier in the relationship. Real love pursues authenticity rather than chasing acceptance.

So here's how I'm challenging myself to break free from people pleasing…I have to make peace with the following realities.

I Can't Please Everyone

Every yes will cost me something. Every no carries with it the potential for disappointment. Either I will disappoint this person by not meeting the full extent of their expectations, or I will disappoint my family by taking too much time from them. Do I wish I could say yes to everything and still keep my sanity? Yes! But I can't. So here's how I will say no:

"Thank you for asking me. My heart says yes, yes, yes, but the reality of my limited time leads me to say no."

A good verse for this is Proverbs 29:25, "Fear of man will prove to be a snare, but whoever trusts in the Lord is kept safe."

I Must Pause Before Giving Immediate Answers

Sometimes it might be realistic for me to say yes, but I've learned to let my yes sit for a spell. Pausing allows me to assess how much stress this will add into my life. The person asking me for this favor probably won't be on the receiving end of my stress. It's the people I love the most who will start getting my worst when I say yes to too many people.

So here's how I will give myself time to make an honest assessment:

"Thank you for asking me. Let me check with my family. If you haven't heard back from me by the end of the week, please connect with me again."

A good verse for this is found in Proverbs 31. Tucked between all the responsibilities the woman in this chapter has is a verse that reveals her attitude. Proverbs 31:25 says, "She is clothed with strength and dignity; she can laugh at the days to come." What this says to me is she doesn't set her heart up to dread what lies ahead.

I Need to Make Peace with the Fact Some People Won't Like Me

In an effort to keep my life balanced, I will have to say no to many things. If someone stops liking me for saying no, they will eventually stop liking me even if I say yes right now.

There are some people I won't please no matter how much I give. And some people won't stop liking me no matter how many no's I give. My true friends are in that second group, and I love them for that.

Here's a great verse for this: "On the contrary, we speak as those approved by God to be entrusted with the gospel. We are not trying to please people but God, who tests our hearts" (1 Thessalonians 2:4).

In the process of learning to say yes to God, we also have to learn to say no to others sometimes. When we pursue radical obedience, we may not be able to make everyone happy along the way. Actually, let me rephrase that—we will *not* be able to make everyone happy along the way. And the sooner we learn to live with this reality, the more authentic our relationships will be.

Someone will probably ask you to add something new to your plate this week, but I'd like to challenge you to take a long pause before giving your final answer. Remember to pursue authenticity by being honest rather than chasing acceptance by always saying yes to others. In this way, we will be able to open our hearts to what God is calling us to do.

> *Dear Lord, thank You for Your Word. I love how it applies to such everyday issues, such as people pleasing. Please help me discern when I should say yes and when I should say no. I want to be a good steward of my time and a good friend/wife/mother/employee, but sometimes I get so caught up in what everyone else wants me to do. Help me to see Your will for each situation and how to respond clearly. In Jesus' name, amen.*

🕊 Reflect and Respond:

How can the practice of pausing before saying yes improve your relationships?

Come up with your predetermined response for saying no. Having a predetermined answer often eases the pressure when responding to others.

28

Attack of the Naysayers

*Am I now trying to win the approval of human beings,
or of God? Or am I trying to please people?
If I were still trying to please people,
I would not be a servant of Christ.*

GALATIANS 1:10

Thought for the Day:

"If my life is fruitless, it doesn't matter who praises me, and if my life is fruitful, it doesn't matter who criticizes me." —John Bunyan

I COULD SEE IT in the cross expression on her face and in the urgency in her stride. The woman approaching me had a few things on her mind.

Sure enough, this woman in my Bible study class thought I was taking my faith a little too seriously and the Bible a little too literally. After she dumped her load of concern on me, she smiled and encouraged me to lighten up. "Honey," she said, "I wouldn't want to see you carry this obedience thing too far."

This, my friend, is a naysayer. If you choose the life of radical obedience, you are going to encounter such people. They don't understand you. They don't want to understand you. And often what you're doing makes them feel convicted. If someone is quick to find fault in something good someone else is doing, that person is usually wrapped up in his or her own self-centered outlook. Naysayers make themselves feel better by tearing others down. Paul warned Timothy about people like this.

> Mark this: There will be terrible times in the last days. People will be lovers of themselves, lovers of money, boastful, proud, abusive, disobedient to their parents, ungrateful, unholy, without love, unforgiving, slanderous, without self-control, brutal, not lovers of good, treacherous, rash, conceited, lovers of pleasure rather than lovers of God—having a form of godliness but denying its power. Have nothing to do with such people (2 Timothy 3:1-5).

Becoming a woman who unashamedly says yes to God is going to cause you to be different from many of your family members and friends. You will examine life's circumstances with a different outlook. You will perceive things with a different expectation. You will understand that just because life is busy doesn't mean you have to rush about without God. You understand your responsibility is to obey God and He will handle the outcome. When you start to fret or worry, you know how to get swept into God's assurance rather than swept away in fear. You will rely on a strength and power that simply does not make sense to most people.

While not all of your friends and family will be naysayers, some will. The difference naysayers see in you compels them to come against you full force because Christ working through you will sometimes step on the toes of their consciences. While naysayers may talk a good Christian game, they deny Christ in their attitudes and actions toward others. Instead of allowing those feelings of conviction to produce good changes in them, they seek to discourage you in hopes of hushing Christ in you.

It's not easy to keep their negativity from being discouraging, but as my husband always reminds me, "Lysa, consider the source." I ask myself, "Is this person criticizing me active in pursuing a relationship with the Lord? Is this person answering God's call on his life, producing the evidence of Christ's fruit? Does he have my best interest in mind?" The answers are almost always no. So I look for any truth that might be in what this person has said, forgive him for any hurt he may have caused, and let the rest go.

What about when the person causing the hurt and becoming a source of discouragement is a strong believer? Even strong believers pursuing God can get pulled into ungodly attitudes. If only people had flashing signs above their heads that gave warning when they were operating in the flesh instead of the Spirit. A wise friend once gave me a real nugget of truth that I think about often. She warned me as I stepped out and determined to say yes to God in all things, "Never let others' compliments go to your head or their criticisms go to your heart."

In his book *The Purpose Driven Life,* author Rick Warren comments on naysayers.

> You will find that people who do not understand your shape for ministry will criticize you and try to get you to conform to what they think you should be doing. Ignore them. Paul often had to deal with critics who misunderstood and maligned his service.

His response was always the same: Avoid comparisons, resist exaggerations, and seek only God's commendation.[1]

Rick then goes on to quote John Bunyan as saying, "If my life is fruitless, it doesn't matter who praises me, and if my life is fruitful, it doesn't matter who criticizes me."

That's so true!

God calls us to keep our eyes on Him, and to focus on who we are in His sight. I will push through. I will say yes to God even in the midst of naysayers.

Dear Lord, help me to live for Your approval while in an environment full of naysayers. I know I am not here to please them, but to please You. Give me the strength I need to be an example for those who are not walking in obedience. In Jesus' name, amen.

🌾 Reflect and Respond:

How do you react when a naysayer questions your beliefs?

Ask God to speak through you when someone tries to shake your foundation. You want to be prepared to stand your ground in the face of opposition.

29

Women Judging Women

God did not send his Son into the world to condemn
the world, but to save the world through him.

John 3:17

🌿 Thought for the Day:

When we judge others, we elevate ourselves past the ability to recognize our own propensity to sin in the very area we are criticizing.

HOW DIFFERENT MIGHT OUR lives be if we didn't have to fear the harsh criticisms of other women? Might we be willing to step out a little bolder for Jesus? A little more vulnerable? A little less guarded? Say yes a little more?

Jesus made it very clear that He didn't come to this world to bring condemnation. He never even condemned the worst of sinners. He leveled His harshest criticisms against those sinners who dared to cast judgments against others.

Oh, sweet sisters, women judging other women must absolutely break God's heart. The crazy thing is when we judge others, we elevate ourselves past the ability to recognize our own propensity to sin in the very area we are criticizing.

Show me a woman who is leveling a judgment against another person, and I will show you a woman who is wrapped in sin herself. If it's not the very same sin she's criticizing, it will be a sin just as dangerous—pride.

It is a subtle shift Satan invites us into. Voicing criticisms against others will coat the eyes of our soul with smut so thick, we become blinded to our own sin. Pride and self-righteousness will detour us from God's best path and lead us on a treacherous journey of denial. We'll deny our own sinfulness. We'll deny our own need for grace.

Those who can't see their own desperate need for grace refuse to freely give grace to others.

Now, if you're like me, you may be tempted to make a mental list of those you have felt judged by, and a few sentences back you started to pray: "Please let so-and-so read today's devotion. I hope she sees herself in this and gets a whammy of conviction."

But let's stop making that mental list and receive this message personally. Even if we are not naturally critical people, this is an area we can all improve on.

I recently read a wonderful quote outlining a beautiful plan when we feel tempted to judge someone else. Francis Frangipane in his book *Holiness, Truth, and the Presence of God* says

> Anyone can pass judgment, but can they save? Can they lay down their lives in love, intercession and faith for the one judged? Can they target an area of need and, rather than criticizing, fast and pray, asking God to supply the very virtue they feel is lacking? And then, can they persevere in love-motivated

prayer until that fallen area blooms in godliness?
Such is the life Christ commands we follow![1]

I know just writing this will not suddenly make the world tip on its axis and shake all of us women into breaking the cycle of criticisms and judgment. However, maybe, it will be a start. If it causes even one of us to fall in front of Jesus in repentance and allow Him to wipe the smut of pride and self-righteousness from our spiritual eyes, it will be a great start. Now, let me be that one.

Dear Lord, forgive me for not extending grace at times to others. I am a woman who desperately needs grace, so I should be a woman who freely offers it. When I am tempted to be critical of someone else, help me hold my thoughts and my tongue. Instead of voicing those things, help me bring them to You in honest and heartfelt prayers for that person. In Jesus' name, amen.

✒ Reflect and Respond:

Is the Lord convicting you of being critical of someone else?

Instead of being critical, let's exercise our right to encourage. Choose someone whom you would normally be critical of and focus on one way you can sincerely encourage her this week.

30

The Unraveling of a Marriage

Be devoted to one another in love.
Honor one another above yourselves.

ROMANS 12:10

🌿 **Thought for the Day:**

Doing what seems easy in the moment often isn't what's best for the long term.

I HAD A FAVORITE sweater I loved wearing. It wasn't too bulky but was still warm and cozy. The only problem was that the threads were loosely woven together. It would snag on things, so I had to be ever so careful when I wore it.

I was always mindful of the delicate nature of this sweater so I could protect it, make it last, and enjoy wearing it time and again.

Then one morning when I was in a hurry, I grabbed some materials I needed for a meeting and rushed to my car. I tossed all my stuff over to the passenger seat, including a spiral notebook. Its metal binding wire caught my sleeve, and as I pulled my arm toward the steering wheel, the notebook came with it and pulled a huge snag in my sweater.

I unhooked myself and assessed the damage. What I should have done was take the sweater off, put something else on, and later taken the time to repair the snag the correct way.

But in the rush of all I had going on, I made the tragic decision to do what seemed easiest in the moment. I snipped the loose threads and hoped for the best. That tragic decision started an unraveling process that ended the life of that beautiful sweater.

Recently, my husband and I got into an argument. In front of the kids. Over something so stupid. And right before we were about to head out the door to go on a date. In the heat of the argument, Art announced the date was off. He no longer wanted to go. And, honestly, I no longer wanted to go either.

Instead, I wanted to go sit in a coffee shop by myself and make a mental list of all the reasons I was right. All the reasons he was wrong. I wanted to justify my perspective.

It's at this exact moment of resistance that an unraveling can begin.

Doing what seems easy in the moment often isn't what's best for the long term.

I pushed for us to still go on our date. It wasn't fun. It wasn't easy. There were tears. There were awkward stretches of silence.

But we pushed through the resistance we both felt and eventually talked. Talked through the snags. The pulls. The things that threaten to unravel us.

There is a delicate nature to marriage. It's so easy to forget that. It's so easy to take it all for granted and stop being careful. Stop being mindful. Stop being protective.

The unraveling can happen so quickly. And the unraveling

doesn't just happen in marriages. It can occur with your best friends, your children, or your in-laws…especially during stressful periods in life.

Be intentional about catching the snags in your relationships. Today. Right now. Say yes to letting God shine through you in these instances, even if you don't feel very cheery or Christian. The Lord has called us to a higher standard that helps to maintain the blessings and people He has placed in our lives. If you continue to lean on your own capabilities, your stubborn desires may create a hole in your dearest relationships. Saying yes to Him will make all the difference.

For me, being intentional required an apology to Art. The right way. By admitting I was wrong and asking for forgiveness. Repairing the snags the right way…tying a knot and tucking it back into the weave of our relationship fabric.

> *Dear Lord, thank You for the special relationships that have been placed in my life. I know I let my emotional state get the best of me sometimes, but I want You to be in control of how I react to situations. Please give me the spirit I need to build up the people around me instead of tearing them down. In Jesus' name, amen.*

🌿 Reflect and Respond:

What's something you can do today to invest wisely in your relationships?

Write down two people you will commit to improving your

relationship with this month. Note things that are special to them, such as favorite hobbies, movies, places to eat, etc. Use this information to bless them in the time you spend together.

1.

2.

31

The Place Where Disappointment Grows

Then you will know that I am the Lord;
those who hope in me will not be disappointed.

Isaiah 49:23

✿ **Thought for the Day:**

The space between our expectations and our reality is a fertile field. It will grow something.

WHEN I WAS IN high school, I had a friend whose sister had the coolest hairdo. It was cropped short with straight bangs that fell messily over one eye. She was that older sister who just seemed to have a handle on how to do everything with style.

I somehow decided all of her coolness traced back to her hairdo. As though that were the budding spot from which the life I wanted could sprout.

Yes, that hairdo.

Never mind the fact her hair was thin and obedient, and mine was thick and rebellious. Never mind that her hair was sleek and straight, and mine was curly at best and frizzy at worst. Never mind that her bangs fell nicely over her forehead, and mine had a crazy cowlick causing them to grow up, not down.

Yes, never mind reality.

I set my expectation on the highest bar and willed my hair to fall in line.

The hairdresser chopped. And chopped. And chopped. And she tried to assure me I now looked JUST like the picture of the older sister.

But that was a lie. I knew it. She knew it.

The space between our expectations and our reality is a fertile field. It will grow something. Disappointment. And, oh how true this has been for me. I still have nightmares of that disastrous hairdo where I wake up desperately grabbing at my head to make sure my hair is still there.

But hair grows back. Bad cuts can be fixed in time. That disappointment can be remedied.

Other situations aren't so easy. Maybe you have some space between a current reality and an unfulfilled expectation. If so, I imagine disappointment can be found growing there.

Psalm 23:1 says, "The LORD is my shepherd, I shall not want" (NASB). The Hebrew word for "want" is *chacer*, meaning "to lack, be without, become empty." So if the Lord is my shepherd, I shall not become empty. I shall not live in a constant state of disappointment where circumstances leak me dry.

But…I do sometimes. And not just with my hair. It's other stuff as well.

Important stuff. How do I let the Lord shepherd me so that the gap between my expectations and reality closes? I ask myself questions. Here are three things we can ask ourselves when faced with disappointment

1. *What do I need to learn?* Maybe God has an appointment for me in the midst of this disappointment. If God wants me to see, learn, know, or grow in some way while I work through this unmet expectation, I have to be open to hear this from Him. Many times God shows me a flaw of mine that needs to be addressed. When I address my flaw, I can more easily adjust my expectations.

2. *Could it be that I'm so concerned with what I don't have, I've forgotten to be thankful for what I do have?* Sometimes, it's not that my reality is bad. It's that I created too much space for disappointment to grow by placing my expectations too high.

3. *Is there something I can do to change this situation?* If so, I need to ask God for the courage to make changes. If I keep hoping things will get better but don't make any adjustments, that's foolish. The space between my reality and my expectations will only change if I do.

When we place our hope in the things of this world, we can expect disappointment to grow. But can I whisper some encouragement to you? Let's look to today's verse, Isaiah 49:23. It holds such a sweet promise—when we place our hope in the Lord, He will never disappoint us.

I'm so thankful for that truth, and for the trials I've gone through that have allowed me to fully embrace it.

One last thing, though. If I ever start flashing pictures of cute pixie haircuts I'm considering getting, somebody remind me of my high school hair debacle. Please. Pretty please. With a dollop of hair gel on top.

> *Dear Lord, thank You for Your constant patience with me. Sometimes I really struggle with feeling disappointed in situations or in people. Please teach me to rely on You in all my expectations instead of looking to people or things to meet my needs. In Jesus' name, amen.*

Reflect and Respond:

Identify one area in your life where you have allowed disappointment to sink in.

Now ask yourself the three questions mentioned in today's devotion:

1. What do I need to learn from this disappointment?

2. Am I so concerned with what I don't have that I've forgotten to be thankful for what I do have?

3. Can I change this situation?

32

I Don't Want to Raise a Good Child

*Start children off on the way they should go,
and even when they are old they will not turn from it.*

PROVERBS 22:6

🌿 Thought for the Day:

Maybe God's goal wasn't for me to raise a good, rule-following child. God's goal was for me to raise a God-following adult.

WHEN MY DAUGHTER HOPE was a senior in high school, she decided her last year should be adventurous and a little out of the "normal" box. A lot out of the box, actually.

She withdrew from traditional school, applied with the state to homeschool, and enrolled in online college courses that would allow her to get both high school and college credit simultaneously. And she planned to spend the month of January serving in Nicaragua doing missions.

This didn't surprise me. Hope has always liked charting her own course.

When she was really little, I was scared to death I was the world's worst mom because Hope was never one to be contained.

And I honestly thought all her extra tenacity was a sign of my poor mothering.

One day I took her to the mall to meet several of my friends with toddlers to grab lunch. All of their kids sat quietly eating Cheerios in their strollers. They shined their halos and quoted Bible verses and used tissues to wipe their noses.

Not Hope.

She was infuriated by my insistence she stay in her stroller. So when I turned away for a split-second to place our lunch order, she wiggled free. She stripped off all her clothes. She ran across the food court. And she jumped in the fountain in the center of the mall.

Nothing makes the mother of a toddler feel more incapable than seeing her naked child splashing in the mall fountain, except maybe that toddler refusing to get out and said mother having to also get into the fountain.

I cried all the way home.

Not because of what she'd done that day, but rather because of how she was every day. So determined. So independent. So insistent.

I would beg God to show me how to raise a good child. One who stayed in her stroller. One who other people would comment about how wonderfully behaved she was. One who made me look good.

But God seemed slow to answer those prayers. So over the years I changed my prayer. "God, help me to raise Hope to be who You want her to be." Emphasis on "God, HELP ME!"

I think I changed my prayers for her because God started to change my heart. I started sensing He had a different plan in mind for my mothering of Hope. Maybe God's goal wasn't for me to raise a good rule-following child. God's goal was for me to raise a God-following adult. An adult just determined and independent and insistent enough to fulfill a purpose He had in mind all along.

Today's verse reminds us we are training children so that when they are old they will not turn away from biblical principles, but rather implement them in their lifelong pursuit of God. Remember, the things that aggravate you about your child today may be the very things that make them great for God's kingdom tomorrow.

I've certainly seen this in raising Hope.

I don't know what mama needs to hear this today, but let me encourage you from the bottom of my heart with four simple mothering perspectives you must hang on to.

1. Don't take too much credit for their good.

2. Don't take too much credit for their bad.

3. Don't try to raise a good child. Raise a God-following adult.

4. As you learn to say yes to God, teach your child to say yes to God.

As with many things in life, these may look a little messy from the outside, but what truly matters is the work God is doing on the inside.

And all the mamas of fountain-dancing children said, "Amen!"

Dear Lord, thank You for entrusting me with the precious responsibility of children. Sometimes I feel completely inadequate to do this job, but You, Lord, are wise and certainly

*knew what You were doing when You chose me to mother my
children. Help me trust the work You are doing in their hearts,
and help me facilitate a life that enables them to say yes to You.
In Jesus' name, amen.*

🌿 Reflect and Respond:

Do you ever find yourself taking too much credit for your children's good and bad behavior? Think about how shifting your focus
from raising a good child to raising a God-following adult will
change the culture of your family.

33

A Young Woman Who Says Yes to God

*Not everyone who says to me, "Lord, Lord," will
enter the kingdom of heaven, but only the one who
does the will of my Father who is in heaven.*

MATTHEW 7:21

🌿 Thought for the Day:

We need to be so busy looking at what God wants, looking at
Him, that everything else becomes less important.

I DISTINCTLY REMEMBER HEARING my local Christian radio
station quoting Billy Graham as once saying, "We can't see the wind,
but we can feel its effects. In the same way, we can't see God, but
we certainly see His effects." How true. The only thing I'd add to
this fabulous quote is that the more we become aware of God's
effects, the more we'll take credit away from happenstance and place
it where it belongs, with God.

A few years ago, I was praying specifically for God to reveal His
activity in each of my children's lives. I knew they were Christians,
but I wanted to see that they each had their own personal relationship with Him. I wanted God to be less about our family tradition

and more about their own experience of Him. In little ways I started to see evidence of God's activity and discipleship springing to life in each of my kids, but the one that really captured my heart and burned a lasting impression in my soul was with my daughter Ashley.

I was speaking at a Ruth Graham and Friends conference out in California. While I was setting up my book table in the lobby of the church, Ashley called me on my cell phone. Immediately, I sensed the heavy emotion in her tone as she tearfully said, "Mom, I need you to pray for me." I stopped what I was doing and walked outside. I assured her I would absolutely pray for her throughout the weekend but that I'd love to pray with her right that minute. I then inquired about what was troubling her. Her answer stunned me.

She was asking for me to pray that she would have the strength to continue a fast she'd started that morning. Two little boys from her school had recently lost their dad to cancer. She told me that God had clearly spoken to her heart and challenged her to pray and fast for that family all day. She did exactly what God had told her to do but now her stomach was really hurting and she was having a hard time.

I checked my watch and calculated that it would be around 9:00 p.m. back home. I encouraged her that sometimes God just intends a fast to be from sunup to sundown and that I was sure He'd be fine with her eating a little something before going to bed. She replied, "Mom, I know exactly what God told me to do and I want to be obedient. I didn't call so you would talk me out of this. I just need for you to pray for me to have the strength to continue."

Just then a wind blew that tousled my hair and my soul. Effects of God. Just what I'd been praying for. Ashley got it! She was more concerned about keeping God's vision clearly in front of her. She was so busy looking at what He wanted, looking at Him, that everything else became less important.

By the time I walked back into that speaking engagement, I looked like a wreck. My hair was windblown, my makeup tear streaked, and my countenance emotional. But my soul was overflowing with the joyful knowledge that my precious daughter was becoming a true disciple, a young woman who says yes to God!

> *Dear Lord, I come to You full of thanks for all of Your effects I see every day. God, I just want to praise You for the ways You so clearly make Yourself known to me. Help me to grow in my journey to become a woman who fearlessly says yes to You. In Jesus' name, amen.*

🌿 **Reflect and Respond:**

Has God been whispering something to you lately? Commit to listening very carefully for a prompting from the Lord. It could come in the form of praying, fasting, or talking with a friend who is also a believer. God chooses to communicate with us in so many different ways.

34

I Was Her

You will call on me and come and pray to me,
and I will listen to you. You will seek me and find me
when you seek me with all your heart.

JEREMIAH 29:12-13

Thought for the Day:

If I want closeness with Jesus, I won't find that in following any-one but Jesus Himself.

I SAW HER COMING across the arena. Deliberately. Intentionally. Her eyes fixed on the stage...on me...on what I must have repre-sented in that moment—a woman who might understand.

Through the crowd, up the stairs, and then across the stage she came until she stood next to me, pressing her shoulder against mine. I was speaking to 6500 women. And there she was, staring out at thousands but pressing into one. Needing more than words.

Later she explained she needed God and thought if she stood close enough to me, she just might be able to feel Him.

I didn't have time to carefully plan what to do. I've never had this happen before. I've never seen this happen. It wasn't even in my scope of possibility.

But there she was.

And there I was.

Two women who simply, desperately need Jesus.

Because I am so hyperaware of my own desperation for Jesus every moment of every day, I simply wrapped my arm around her and kept on speaking. It was a wrinkle in time. Something that wasn't supposed to be and yet was. And I think I now know why.

I needed to remember that ravenous longing I once had to press against somebody who knew Jesus. I was her. Looking at other people's faith and wondering how to get that. That depth. That closeness. That unswerving conviction.

I truly thought if only a person with that faith would let me close enough, I'd discover their secret. Their formula of faith. I'd learn their routines. I'd mimic their obedience. I'd follow them to the ends of the earth until I got it right. Then, then, then I'd feel close to Jesus. I'd understand the Bible. I'd pray powerful prayers. And all would finally make sense.

However, there is a big difference between being close to people who love Jesus and being close to Jesus Himself.

I can certainly learn from people. "Walk with the wise and become wise" (Proverbs 13:20). But if I want closeness with Jesus, I won't find that in following anyone but Jesus Himself. He is the One who must be pursued.

A thousand whispers have come from my heart. *Show me, Jesus. Show me how to follow You, be close to You, press into You, be more like You…show me. Show me today. Show me in this minute. Show me. Please, Jesus, show me.*

And there will surely be thousands more that pour from my lips. For Jesus wants us to walk with Him. He says "Follow Me" more than 20 times in the Gospels. "Follow Me. Follow Me."

And those who dare to whisper *yes* and then walk in His ways find the One for whom they are longing. "Then you will call on me and come and pray to me, and I will listen to you. You will seek me and find me when you seek me with all your heart" (Jeremiah 29:12-13).

Yes, there she was. And there I was. Two women who simply, desperately need Jesus.

Dear Lord, I just want to feel Your presence. My heart desires to be close to You and to be more like You. Would You show me how to follow You right now, in this moment? I love You, Lord. In Jesus' name, amen.

✐ Reflect and Respond:

There is a big difference between being close to people who love Jesus and being close to Jesus Himself. Take time with these questions:

Am I following Jesus or am I following others more?

How can I seek closeness with Jesus?

Read the book of John in the New Testament to learn more about the life and heartbeat of Jesus Himself. Read where He walked, how He walked, and what He said. It will change your life. Pray to find that closeness for which you've been looking.

35

Ruined for Good

"I am the Lord's servant," Mary answered.
"May your word to me be fulfilled."

LUKE 1:38

Thought for the Day:

God is so perfectly capable of making sure every person hears, knows, and is told, "You are Mine."

ONE NIGHT I TOOK Hope to a gathering of people who have a passion for missions work in Ethiopia. I have to admit, I was really tired and the drive across town sounded even farther than usual, but Hope had a true desire to be at this event.

She had just returned from Ethiopia and desperately wanted to go back. Having just come back from Ethiopia herself, my friend Renee told me that if Hope wanted to go back, I should rest assured it was absolutely a calling from God.

So off we went. And I heard two stories that night that had a lasting impact on my view of radical, blind obedience.

Life is not easy in Ethiopia, but God has shown His face in a mighty way to the people of that country. Two Ethiopian men named Berhanu and Ephrim shared their life stories, and I couldn't stop the tears that forced their way down my cheeks. Berhanu was saved through a vision where Jesus spoke three simple things into his heart: "You are a sinner. You are Mine. I want to use you to tell the nations about Me."

Can you imagine? He wasn't in church. He wasn't surrounded by praise and worship to set just the right tone. There wasn't a pastor giving just the right sermon. He was in a desperate land surrounded by Muslims where Christians are persecuted in horrific ways. And Jesus came to him and said, "You, Berhanu, are Mine."

Amazing. And Berhanu has been walking in the Lord's calling for his life ever since. He keeps sharing his story with those who will listen. It's a story that is hard for many to grasp as we rest in the safety of our American suburbs.

I will remember Berhanu's story every time a skeptic says, "How can Jesus require that all believe in Him to have eternal life when some live in remote places where the name of Jesus will never be spoken?"

God is so perfectly capable of making sure every person hears, knows, and is told, "You are Mine."

Ephrim came to know Jesus while wrongly imprisoned. Prisons in third world countries are the lowliest of places with the most desperate conditions. He couldn't even describe the conditions to us. But in the midst of living a nightmare, a group of Christians in the prison had incredible joy shining from their faces. Ephrim saw, inquired, and eventually believed.

After he got out of prison, he wandered into an AIDS orphanage one day. In the corner of the room something caught his attention.

It was a two-year-old boy, lying on a small, makeshift bed, dying. He was encircled by a group of boys ages 4 to 6, who were holding hands and singing their brother into heaven.

In that instant, Ephrim knew he was ruined for good. He vowed the rest of his days on this earth would be spent telling the children of his destitute country about Jesus. He vowed he would give his life for these kids.

Wow. What amazing stories full of obedience and a true desire to say yes to God's calling. Although these men faced hardships that we could never even begin to imagine, they were touched by the Lord and had a passion to live in Him.

I'm here today to tell you that we can live in that same passion. We can be fully submerged in radical obedience like Ephrim and Berhanu.

And to think I didn't feel like driving across town that night! There is so much power in saying yes to God. He will fully bless our obedience.

Dear Lord, thank You for being a Father to those all over the globe. Give me bigger eyes and a bigger heart to see this world You love so much. I want to be like these men. I want to be radically obedient. In Jesus' name, amen.

Reflect and Respond:

As you were reading the devotion, did the Lord stir something in your heart? Maybe it was a passion you had as a young girl, or maybe it is a new passion. Write it down, even if it seems like a long-forgotten dream. You never know to what or where the Lord is calling you. It may be to Africa, or it may be to your neighbor's house. No matter where, are you ready to say yes?

36

He Chose to Be Unafraid

Pray also for me, that whenever I speak, words
may be given me so that I will fearlessly
make known the mystery of the gospel.

EPHESIANS 6:19

Thought for the Day:

It's amazing to see what can happen when one person dares to say, "I'm going to say yes to God's wild invitation. I'm going to do this."

HAVE YOU EVER HAD one of those amazing thoughts of something you want to do? Your heart beats wildly for a few minutes—or even a few days—and you think to yourself, *I'm going to do this!*

But then the reasons *you can't* start coming. They suit up, start marching, and aim their weapons of discouragement right at your heart. In the end, the amazing thought becomes a fleeting thought.

And you think to yourself, *Yeah, it was a dumb idea.* Then, as quickly as the stir of passion started, it fades. Too many of us live in the depressing, washed-out shades of a thousand faded passions that might have been.

Because we're afraid.

We'd rather stay safe and under the radar than go big and possibly flop big.

But every now and then someone rare comes along. They would rather die than say, "I wish I would have…" Instead, they grit their teeth, lift their raw souls to God, and scream above all the naysayers, "I will! By God, I will!"

That's my pastor.

Never have I seen someone so willing to FEARLESSLY make known the mystery of the gospel than Pastor Steven Furtick. He walks, talks, eats, sleeps, and breathes Ephesians 6:19, "Pray also for me, that whenever I speak, words may be given me so that I will fearlessly make known the mystery of the gospel."

My pastor had a crazy thought fly into his brain to do an old-school revival for 12 nights at the beginning of 2012. One where it wouldn't be about a church and a preacher but one that would be about THE CHURCH with many preachers. One that would be all about getting the hope of Jesus to the masses.

It was a good idea. But it was a crazy idea. What about the expense? What if it burned out the staff? Would people really show up for all 12 nights? So many questions begging the idea to just fade away.

But Pastor Steven didn't let it fade. He didn't let it die. He ignited it. Not because he didn't feel the pull of fear, but rather because he pressed into God and chose to be unafraid.

This crazy thought turned into an amazing reality—Code Orange Revival. Twelve straight nights. Twelve amazing messages. Twelve passionate preachers. One awe-inspiring purpose—to fearlessly make known the mystery of the gospel.

My husband and I had the privilege to attend much of this

revival in person. And though I'm a woman of many words, I can't possibly begin to describe what God did.

There was an igniting of souls that happened and extended all across the globe. People came to know Jesus. People got baptized. People found hope again. And people saw what can happen when one person dares to say, "I'm going to say yes to God's wild invitation. I'm going to do this!"

And then does.

You may be thinking, *My yes can't affect others like this. I don't have that kind of influence.* But, my sweet friend, we cannot even begin to understand the plans God has for us. There is always a far-reaching ripple effect when a woman says yes to God. We don't have to see the spread of the influence to know it's there. The power of saying yes to God is beyond anything we could ever imagine.

Dear Lord, thank You for the examples of great men and women You have placed in our lives. May we humble ourselves as we learn from their courage to say yes to Your call. Give me the strength and courage necessary to take that next step in Your will for me. In Jesus' name, amen.

🌿 Reflect and Respond:

Think of an example of someone who has chosen to say yes to God no matter what the cost. He or she may be in your life now or in your past.

What can you learn from their example of faith and radical obedience?

37

Five Things to Help You Stop Thinking and Start Doing

*Now to him who is able to do immeasurably more than
all we ask or imagine, according to his power that is at
work within us, to him be glory in the church and in
Christ Jesus throughout all generations, for ever and ever!*

EPHESIANS 3:20-21

Thought for the Day:

Taking challenges head-on won't always be pretty, but going to
the Lord for comfort and motivation will keep you going.

MY HUSBAND, ASKED IF I would do a 21-day cleanse with him.
I wasn't excited. I thought, *I already eat pretty healthy. And 21 days is
a really long time to eat like a rabbit. Plus, I don't want to make a commitment I won't keep.*

So I gave him a safe answer: "I'll think about it." And, honestly,
that's all I would have done had he not asked me 217 more times.

Have you ever said "I'll think about it" and still found yourself
"thinking about it" months later? Me too. But I didn't want this to

be another challenge where I just thought about it. I wanted to be able to say, "I did it! I finally did it!" I knew I needed to place my trust in the Lord to help me accomplish this—and He was faithful.

I wonder if you are tired of just thinking and are ready to accomplish some things you've been putting off. If so, I'd love to share what I learned. Here are five crucial things you can do to stop thinking and start doing.

1. Surround Yourself with Success

Get around others who are doing that thing you need to do. Hearing Art talk about and prepare for the cleanse made it more front and center in my life. Being around people who are doing what you need to do makes the first move less scary. And they can help you push through the not-so-fun times.

Remember to pray and connect with God daily. This is key to developing a healthy attitude. Taking challenges head-on won't always be pretty, but going to the Lord for comfort and motivation is what kept me going.

2. Stock Up for Success

Art and I went to grocery stores that carry healthy foods to stock our refrigerator with everything we'd need to be successful. Now, I wish I could say this trip was without conflict. It was not. He wanted to spend what seemed like hours making out a list. I'm emotionally allergic to spending hours making out a list. Just take the list provided in the instruction book and get what you need, for heaven's sake.

Ahem.

Anyhow, no matter what your new thing is, chances are you'll need supplies to invest in your success.

3. Schedule for Your Success

Before we started the cleanse, we found a 21-day time period when several of our kids would be away during a school break (which meant I didn't have to prepare food for others). You'd better believe I did a happy dance over that.

It's important to schedule whatever you're tackling and keep this appointment. Be diligent about not letting life crowd out this important commitment. Set a start date. Track your progress with mini goals. Set a completion date with a reward built in to keep you motivated.

4. Share Your Success

As you have successes, share them with your friends. They may get excited and join in too! During the 21-day process, I told a friend I drank both my cleanse smoothies with only one dramatic gag. This was a big accomplishment! At the end of our conversation, she said she'd like to join me.

How cool! I went from being a moper to a motivator. And that propelled me to keep going.

5. Stretch Your Success

Once you've accomplished your one thing, you'll have GREAT momentum. Use this to help you tackle something else you've been putting off.

While it might feel as though you can't face this big challenge, I want to encourage you. Ephesians 3:20-21 teach that God's mighty power is at work within us. Many times we try to do things alone and work solely within our limitations as humans.

The Lord wants us to lean on Him. To ask for help to do the impossible.

I know it might be hard, but we need to bravely claim God's promise to accomplish infinitely more than we might ask or think.

With God's Spirit in us, I know we will be able to say, "I did it! I finally did it!"

Dear Lord, I'm grateful for this chance to lean on You. Equip me with Your strength as I face my biggest challenges. I'm holding tight to Your promise that all things are possible with Your Spirit in me. In Jesus' name, amen.

🌿 Reflect and Respond:

Is God calling you to face a challenge in your life?

Write down one challenge you'd like to tackle. Create an action plan. Use the five tips above to formulate the steps you'll take to create motivation.

38

Peace like a River

If only you had paid attention to my commands,
your peace would have been like a river,
your well-being like the waves of the sea.

ISAIAH 48:18

 Thought for the Day:

When we focus our minds and fix our attention on Christ, He is magnified and made bigger in our lives.

LET'S BE HONEST. LIFE can get pretty hectic. Between kids' schedules, dinner preparations, and other time commitments, sometimes I can't even remember what a quiet, peaceful house feels like. It's in those moments that God humbles me to lean back and worship Him for all He is.

If I am ever going to find peace past the naysayers, past the attacks of Satan, and past my own weariness, it will only be because I choose daily to walk in absolute obedience to the moment-by-moment, day-by-day, assignment-by-assignment commands of the Lord.

In our verse today, the prophet Isaiah writes, "If only you had paid attention to my commands, your peace would have been like a river, your well-being like the waves of the sea" (Isaiah 48:18). Did you catch the treasure hidden here? One of the most radical blessings for the woman saying yes to God is the peace that rushes through the soul of the one who is attentive to the Lord's commands.

God chose such a unique word to describe His peace—a river! A river is not calm and void of activity. It is active and cleansing and confident of the direction it is headed in. It doesn't get caught up with the rocks in its path. It flows over and around them, all the while smoothing their jagged edges and allowing them to add to its beauty rather than take away from it. A river is a wonderful thing to behold.

Beth Moore says, "To have peace like a river is to have security and tranquility while meeting the many bumps and unexpected turns on life's journey. Peace is submission to a trustworthy Authority, not resignation from activity."[1]

Jesus tells us His peace is unlike the world's peace: "Peace I leave with you; my peace I give you. I do not give to you as the world gives. Do not let your hearts be troubled and do not be afraid" (John 14:27). The world's way to peace would have me pull back to make life a little easier for me, my circumstances, and my family. The problem with this is that we were not put here to be all about ourselves—we were put here to be all about God. We are to die to our self-centeredness so we can have more of Christ in our hearts and minds.

Jesus clearly tells us to focus on Him, His ways, and His example, and His peace will be with us. The focus of our hearts and minds will shape our decisions and actions that follow: "You [God] will keep in perfect peace those whose minds are steadfast, because they trust in you" (Isaiah 26:3).

When we focus our minds and fix our attention on Christ, He is magnified and made bigger in our lives. When we focus our minds and fix our attention on life's obstacles, they will be wrongly magnified and made to appear larger than they really are. Our attention is like a magnifying glass—whatever we place it on becomes larger and more consuming of our time and energy. We desire to focus on Christ alone but sometimes other things seem bigger, and so, without even realizing it, we shift our focus. Before we know it, we are drawn into the muck and mire on the outer banks of Jesus' river of peace.

But sometimes it is down on your face in the mud in complete humility (and perhaps even humiliation!) that you will find a sweet and tender truth. It's from this position that you can say, "Jesus, I love You and want You more than anything else. I love You and want You more than the approval of my peers, family and friends, and even the naysayers in my life. I love You and want You more than the comforts and trappings of this world. I love You and choose to believe Your truth over Satan's lies. I love You and choose to worship You and You alone. Jesus, I love You and want to come to You empty handed and offer my life in complete surrender."

Saying yes to God is a lot more about being than doing. It is choosing whom I will worship and then depending on God to give me the strength to follow through.

As my soul looks up from life's muck and rights the focus of its attention, I find myself pressing back into the river, where Jesus' peace rushes over me, refreshing, cleansing, and invigorating.

Dear Lord, I am so grateful for the peace You provide for me. I adore You and want to focus my mind and attention on You today and every day. In Jesus' name, amen.

Reflect and Respond:

Do you find yourself in constant need of God's peace? Come into God's presence today and seek His peace over your life. Pray diligently that He will cover your household and relationships in His blessings and protection from the discouragement of life's obstacles.

39

A Little Girl's Dance

I lift up my eyes to the mountains—
where does my help come from?
My help comes from the LORD,
the Maker of heaven and earth.

PSALM 121:1-2

Thought for the Day:

My steps so often betray the desire of my heart, but it is not my perfect performance that captures His attention.

MY TOUCH HAS ALWAYS comforted my youngest daughter, Brooke.

I can remember running errands when she was a baby, knowing we should have been home an hour earlier for her nap. But also knowing there were things that had to get done, I pressed on, hoping for the best. She started getting fussy, which made everyone else in the car start to lose patience. One of my older daughters, feeling very wise at five years old, said, "Mom, just tell her to stop crying. Tell her she'll get in big trouble if she doesn't."

Well, that might make a toddler who wouldn't want to miss out on watching *Barney* that afternoon settle down, but it did not work with a baby. She wanted to get out of that car, and she wanted to make sure we all knew it. What started as some whines and whimpers soon escalated into a full-blown meltdown complete with tears, wailing, and screaming.

I couldn't do much to comfort her while trying to drive, but I could reach my arm into the backseat and gently pat her leg. It took a few minutes, but eventually she settled down and reached out her tiny hand to hold mine.

When Brooke was older but still a young girl, she had a performance with her praise dance team from school. The girls looked especially beautiful that day dressed all in white, their hair pulled gently back from their faces, and each had an extra measure of grace in their step. I couldn't wait to see Brooke perform these dances she'd been working on and talking about for weeks. She loved getting up on a stage, so I expected her to be full of smiles and giggles. But just a few minutes before the performance was about to begin, a very distraught Brooke made her way to the audience to find me.

With tears streaming down her cheeks, she explained that the teacher had moved her from the front row to the back row, and she didn't know the back row's part. I assured her everything would be fine. I whispered, "Honey, just get up there and watch the other girls for cues and follow in step. You know this dance, Brooke. You'll be fine."

She sobbed back, "I won't be fine if I mess up, and I know I'm going to mess up."

That's when it occurred to me. She would need my touch to get through this. But she and I both knew it would not be possible for my arm to reach all the way up to the stage. So I quickly whispered, "Brooke, lock your eyes with mine, and Mommy will touch you with my smile. Don't look at anyone or anything else. Don't even look at the other girls dancing. It doesn't matter if you mess up. What matters is that you keep your eyes on me the whole time. We'll do this together."

Quietly she asked, "The whole time, Mommy?"

"The whole time, Brooke," I replied as I watched my brave girl walk away to take her place in line.

Several times during the dance, Brooke fell out of step. Her arms would go down when the rest of the back row lifted theirs up. She would go left and bump into the others headed right. She knew her steps weren't perfect, so her eyes brimmed with tears. However, the tears never fell. With her eyes perfectly locked on my smiling face, she danced.

She danced when the steps came easy.

She danced when her steps got jumbled.

She danced even when her emotions begged her to quit.

She danced the whole way through.

She danced and I smiled.

I smiled when her steps were right on track. I smiled when they weren't.

My smile was not based on her performance. My smile was born out of an incredible love for this precious, courageous little girl. As she kept her attention focused solely on my smile and the touch of my gaze, it was as if the world slowly faded away and we were the only ones in the room.

This is the way God wants me to dance through life.

Though I can't physically see Him, my soul pictures Him so clearly. In my mind's eye He is there. The touch of His gaze wraps about me, comforts me, assures me, and makes the world seem strangely dim. As long as my gaze is locked on His, I dance and He smiles. The snickers and jeers of others fade away. Though I hear their razor-sharp intentions, they are unable to pierce my heart and distract my focus. Even my own stumblings don't cause the same feelings of defeat.

My steps so often betray the desire of my heart, but it is not my perfect performance that captures His attention. Rather, it is my complete dependence on Him that He notices.

He then whispers, "Hold on to Me and what I say about you. For My words are the truth of who you are and the essence of what you were created to be." I then imagine Him pausing and, with tears in His eyes and a crack in His voice, He adds, "Then you will know the truth, and the truth will set you free" (John 8:32).

His truth frees you from the chains of doubt and despair. His truth frees me from feeling unable and inadequate to try and pursue God in an all-out way. His truth washes over me as I tentatively whisper, "I want to be a woman who says yes to God."

And in that moment, with my eyes locked on His, I am.

Dear Lord, I want to keep my eyes on You as I dance through the highs and lows of my life. Show me Your truth today as I pursue You, and soften my heart so that I may completely depend on You instead of myself. In Jesus' name, amen.

Reflect and Respond:

Do you feel as though you have inadequacies and shortcomings that keep you from fully pursuing God? He wants us to keep our eyes on Him so we can break free from these chains of self-doubt.

Take some time to reflect on verses where God says who we are to Him, such as Ephesians 1:3-8, 2 Corinthians 1:21-22, and John 1:12.

40

The Unsaved Christian

The LORD your God is with you,
the Mighty Warrior who saves.
He will take great delight in you;
in his love he will no longer rebuke you,
but will rejoice over you with singing.

ZEPHANIAH 3:17

Thought for the Day:

My imperfections are safely tucked within the reality of His perfection.

ONE SATURDAY I WAS speaking at a conference. While I was there, I met a beautiful woman about my age. I don't know many details about her life. I don't know if she is single or married…if she has kids or not…if she works outside the home or in her home. But what I do know is she's been going to church for a long time.

Not only has she been going, but she's been involved through serving, giving, and doing all the right church stuff.

Yet something was missing.

"I never could quite put my finger on it until this weekend," she whispered. "I never knew what it really meant to have a relationship with Jesus. But hearing you explain it, something clicked. I walked forward today. I gave my heart to Jesus."

She brushed her long dark hair away from her eyes, and I could see the sparkle, the joy, the realization of salvation. Scattered pieces of faith coming together to make the picture of Jesus more clear, more solid, more applicable in her life.

A fresh vision of hope.

I wondered which part of what I shared made this profound click happen in her soul. Of course, it was the Holy Spirit moving, but somehow in the midst of me sharing the broken places of my life, things came together in hers.

It got me thinking about us Jesus girls doing life together. A few moments whispering truths back and forth online or in Bible study groups learning how to navigate life as Jesus girls. But all that we talk about is for nothing if our hearts stay far from Jesus.

It's not about momentary motivation to make it through today.

It's not about spiffy quotes to ponder and put into practice.

It's not about relationship tactics and turnkey solutions.

It's not about bite-sized pieces of peace to make life a little more manageable.

It's not about making our lives look and feel a little better.

It has to be about Jesus.

And drawing our hearts into His reality. His grace. His love. His hope. His forgiveness. And, most of all, drawing our hearts into the free gift of salvation because of Him.

God doesn't want us to have a religion. A religion is where we follow rules hoping to do life right, and we serve God out of duty because we think we have to. God wants us to have a relationship where we follow Him. And we serve God not out of duty but out of delight because of the realization of who we are in Him.

For years I defined myself as the broken child of a broken daddy. I went to church to get a little "God goodness" in my life, but it was like putting fresh paint on rotting wood. I was living just like those talked about in Isaiah 29:13, "The Lord says: 'These people come near to me with their mouth and honor me with their lips, but their hearts are far from me. Their worship of me is based on merely human rules they have been taught.'"

It took me a long time to realize I didn't have to be defined by the circumstances of my life. I could be defined by the reality of who God says I am. I wasn't a broken child of a broken daddy…I was a forgiven and loved child of the Most High God…my heavenly Father.

I didn't need a little "God goodness" to rub off on me. I needed God to invade the deepest parts in me.

I didn't need to be just following the rules. I needed to be following God Himself.

So I knelt down in the midst of my messy, chaotic, confused life, and I started a relationship with Him by simply saying yes.

Yes, I am a sinner in need of a Savior.

Yes, I acknowledge Jesus Christ as the Son of God, sent to die on a cross and be resurrected on the third day to save me from my sins.

Yes, I want Jesus to be the Lord and Master of my life.

Yes, now and forever I will be a forgiven and saved child of the Almighty God.

Yes, I will follow Jesus today, tomorrow, and every day I'm blessed to be on this earth.

Oh sister, let me quiet the voice of Satan screaming to resist this process because you won't be able to live this out perfectly. Jesus has never ever asked for us to be perfect. He simply wants us perfectly surrendered. I often pray, *Oh Jesus, I am such a mess, but I am Yours. Show me…help me…forgive me…reassure me…and pour Your tender mercy upon me.*

And He does. He always will.

My imperfections are safely tucked within the reality of His perfection. And I simply press on by continuing to say YES moment by imperfect moment, day by imperfect day.

Dear Lord, I praise You today for Your power to redeem me from all of my sins. Words can't even begin to describe how thankful I am for Your protection over my life. Guide my steps and thoughts as I continue to live in You. In Jesus' name, amen.

🌿 Reflect and Respond:

Who could you share the gospel with today?

Reflect on your own walk with the Lord and use lessons you've learned to speak life into a friend.

Notes

Chapter 3—Hearing God's Voice

1. *Life Application Study Bible (NIV)* (Wheaton, IL: Tyndale House Publishers, 1988), 2125.

Chapter 4—God's Calling

1. Rick Warren, *The Purpose Driven Life* (Grand Rapids, MI: Zondervan Publishing House, 2002), 233.

Chapter 14—No Matter What

1. A.J. Russell, ed., *God Calling* (Grand Rapids, MI: Spire Books, 2005), May 19.

Chapter 15—The Power to Obey

1. *Life Application Study Bible (NIV)* (Wheaton, IL: Tyndale House Publishers, 1998), 2277.

Chapter 28—Attack of the Naysayers

1. Rick Warren, *The Purpose Driven Life* (Grand Rapids, MI: Zondervan Publishing House, 2002), 254.

Chapter 29—Women Judging Women

1. Francis Frangipane, *Holiness, Truth and the Presence of God* (Cedar Rapids, IA: Arrow Publications, 1986), 11.

Chapter 38—Peace like a River

1. Beth Moore, *Living Free* (Nashville, TN: LifeWay Press, 2001), 82.

More Lysa Terkeurst Books
from Harvest House Publishers

What Happens When Women Say Yes to God

What Happens When Women Say Yes to God DVD

*What Happens When Women Say Yes to God
Interactive Workbook*

What Happens When Young Women Say Yes to God

Am I Messing Up My Kids?

Other Great Reads
from Lysa Terkeurst

Finding I AM

Uninvited

The Best Yes

Becoming More Than a Good Bible Study Girl

Unglued

Made to Crave

Made to Crave for Young Women

About Proverbs 31 Ministries

Lysa TerKeurst is the president of Proverbs 31 Ministries, located in Charlotte, North Carolina.

If you were inspired by *What Happens When Women Say Yes to God* and desire to deepen your own personal relationship with Jesus Christ, we have just what you're looking for.

Proverbs 31 Ministries exists to be a trusted friend who will take you by the hand and walk by your side, leading you one step closer to the heart of God through:

Free First 5 app
Free online daily devotions
Online Bible studies
Writer and speaker training
Daily radio programs
Books and resources

For more information about Proverbs 31 Ministries,
visit www.Proverbs31.org.

To inquire about having Lysa speak at your event,
visit www.LysaTerKeurst.com and click on "speaking."

About Lysa

Lysa TerKeurst is president of Proverbs 31 Ministries and the *New York Times* bestselling author of *The Best Yes*, *Unglued*, *Made to Crave*, and 16 other books.

As president of Proverbs 31 Ministries, Lysa and her team have led thousands to make their walk with God an invigorating journey through daily online devotionals, radio programs, online Bible studies, speaker/writing training, and more.

Lysa was recently awarded the Champions of Faith Author Award and has been published in multiple publications such as *Focus on the Family* and CNN online. Additionally, she has appeared on the *Today Show* as one of the leading voices in the Christian community.

Each year, Lysa is a featured keynote presenter at more than 40 events across North America, including the Women of Joy Conferences and the Catalyst Leadership Conference. She has a passion for equipping women to share their stories for God's glory through Proverbs 31 Ministries' annual She Speaks Conference and writer training program, COMPEL: Words That Move People.

Lysa's personal adventure of following God captured national media attention when their family adopted two teenage boys from a war-torn orphanage in Liberia, Africa. They never imagined their decision would start a chain reaction within their community, which inspired other families to adopt more than 45 children from the same orphanage! Lysa's amazing story led to appearances on *The Oprah Winfrey Show*, *Good Morning America*, *The 700 Club*, *USA Today* newspaper, *Woman's Day* magazine, and *Focus on the Family* radio.